D1287758

Wood Design

WOOD DESIGN
by Donald Willcox

Watson-Guptill Publications / New York

Wall I by Jane Teller, 1959. 5′8″ high, 4′3″ long, and 20″ deep; a construction of textures in Oak, Walnut, and Chestnut. Contrast to create emphasis here draws the eye almost immediately to the rounded middle section of this wall. It seems impossible to penetrate this wall, a feeling that is gained through repetition in the building of horizontal layers, each with a unique texture. Photo by Werner Goodwin; courtesy The American Craftsman's Council and the artist.

First published 1968 in the United States and Canada by Watson-Guptill Publications,
a division of Billboard Publications, Inc.,
One Astor Plaza, New York, N.Y. 10036

Published 1974 in Great Britain by Sir Isaac Pitman & Sons Ltd.,
39 Parker Street, Kingsway, London WC2B 5PB
ISBN 0-273-00895-1

Manufactured in U.S.A.

ISBN 0-8230-5850-6

Library of Congress Catalog Card Number: 68-12400

First Printing, 1968
Second Printing, 1969
Third Printing, 1970
Fourth Printing, 1972
Fifth Printing, 1974

To my *illustrator, and mother of our three daughters.*

Acknowledgments

The author scribbled the words, but many people helped in the making of this book. I thank them all, some by name: Susan Meyer, my editor; Dave Congalton for expert photography; Brad Smith, Einars Mengis, and the Shelburne Museum Staff; Jean Godsman, and The American Craftsman's Council; Elizabeth Little, and the Museum of Primitive Art; Richard Tooke, and The Museum of Modern Art; Fred McDarrah, Jonas Lehrman, Wendell Castle, Pat Nachman, Adele Miller, and the Breadloaf Writer's Conference for inspiration and advice; and the many sculptors and galleries who gave me time, resources, and the use of photographs. And I thank, too, the many people who had to live with and around me while I worked.

Swordsman whirligig, circa 1870. 18″ high.
An early example of functional kinetics. The arms
of this wind toy swing back and forth and it pivots
on the base as the wind blows. Photo by Einars J.
Mengis; courtesy Shelburne Museum, Inc.

Contents

". . . Fold up your aprons, craftsmen, cast your tools away, fling off Necessity's firm yoke, for Freedom calls. Freedom, my lads, is neither wine nor a sweet maid, not goods stacked in vast cellars, no, nor sons in cradles; it's but a scornful, lonely song the wind has taken . . ."

The Odyssey, A Modern Sequel
by Nikos Kazantzakis

Introduction

This is not a copybook! It's a vigorous attempt to stimulate original design; *your own* original design in wood. As the author, it's my job to reach you, to poke my arm right out from this page and give you a shove, a hefty, but loving prod toward discovering what you can do yourself in exploring the possibilities of design in wood. There are no patterns included with this book because I don't want you to copy. I want you to tap your own resources; discover the flowing energy of your own imagination. It's right there! Yes, even in *you*! And my task is to reach you—visually and verbally—through this book.

If you thought you were buying just another "carve-by-the-numbers" book, you won't find it here. When you produce something "carved-by-the-numbers," you haven't created anything; you've simply followed directions, and proved to yourself what you already know: that you can read.

The illustrations

Visually I'm going to let you sit right at home and give you an armchair tour through several outstanding museum collections, and then take you through a number of contemporary art galleries to let you see what's happening currently in wood design.

This cover-to-cover gallery of ours will span the spectrum of design from primitive to abstract. The selection of photographs is entirely my own. I'm trying to prove a point visually. I'm trying to show you (with a minimum of inconsistency) that a design doesn't have to be cluttered, Victorian, embellished with gargoyles, gimcracks, and all manner of excess confusion to be a work of art. I'm trying to show you that more often than not, the simplest and cleanest design in wood is the most effective. The photographs will run from primitive wood design, to American folk carvings, and finally to contemporary design and the current use of new materials and techniques. I'm trying to prove to you visually that there is a blood relationship between the child-like simplicity expressed in

Wig stand Painted Pine carved in the round. Used strictly as a display stand for wigs. Compare it with William King's *Bust of a young woman* on page 120 for a contemporary extension of this same design. Photo by Einars J. Mengis; courtesy Shelburne Museum Inc.

primitive and American folk carving, and the straightforward, uncluttered statement of the most contemporary craftsman. We're cleaning up our designs, hacking off the doodads, and returning to the vision of simplicity. It's as if we were seeing the world with the *real* raw materials of our sensory perception.

The photographs in the book have been selected to cover a broad cross section in the use of wood as a design medium; from a mobile to a weather vane, from a wall hanging in relief to a chess set, from a carved chest to something architecturally ornamental. I'm attempting to present a maximum number of ideas which can be applied to the design of a given piece of wood. Quietly I'm saying: "Here's a piece of wood. Realize its design potential before you consume it."

Definitions

A book of this type attempts to verbalize the creative process, and this is a very uncertain task. A book uses words to communicate with the reader. Words cannot substitute for experience. How much better it would be for both of us if I could sit you down beside me in my studio or, better yet, charge the nerve endings of your fingertips and of your heart. I could then lead you to a piece of Henry Moore's sculpture and say: "Feel it. Go ahead. Stand back and let that piece swallow you. How do you react to it?" And then, if we were communicating emotionally, I wouldn't have to give you words. You'd have tucked away the experience inside you, where special things go, and you would have grown artistically.

There is an ever-present danger of ambiguity when translating an act of doing (or an emotional experience) into words. A given word may stimulate a spectrum of mental images, each quite different in meaning. Two people talking about *craft* may lose touch because each person is using his own definition. *Craft* in this text means skill, or competence in using tools. *Technique* is the way in which the tool is applied to a given piece of wood in one of several methods, as for example, one *technique* is sculpture, while a second *technique* is relief carving.

Design, the strongest word in the text, can connote many things, from the surface decoration on a colonial carved chest, to the silhouette of an outdoor Henry Moore against a Montreal skyline; from the texture of rough adz marks on an Indian totem-pole, to the composition of a delicate suspended mobile. The Greek word for design means poetry. Perhaps we can best span the meaning of design by calling it a harmonious marriage of art and order. In this text, *design* is the "thing," the project, the representation in space that the artist attempts to capture.

Techniques in wood design

The book suggests a number of techniques: it gives the reader an opportunity to tiptoe unnoticed into the studio of the professional and look over his shoulder. Techniques may seem a bore, but they are not. The mastery over tools, and the use of one's hands are skills that are absolutely necessary to make ideas come alive. Creating is not limited to ideas; just *thinking* of an interesting design does not make it a visual reality.

An introduction to the traditional techniques of sculpture, relief, incised, pierced, and chip carving are included in the text. The book also reaches beyond these traditional techniques and moves into the areas of construction, lamination, painted sculpture, with enough on steaming and bending to tickle your curiosity if this technique should interest you.

The techniques presented will try and answer the question of how, rather than providing precise procedures step-by-step. I've assumed the reader is intelligent and interested so I have explained the techniques loosely, with simplicity, and from a practical—rather than an academic point of view—knowing that most of technique comes from practice and not (unfortunately) from printed black letters on a white page. Other chapters will suggest ways to set up your studio, introduce you to tools and their use, discuss wood and its characteristics, the principles of design, and various kinds of finishes.

Features of design

From a seed of internal vision, a design in wood is built into an external reality. There is a deep, lush feeling in having created something unique; in being the producer of the seed that has taken life through your own hands and has grown into something pleasing to the eye and to the senses. Original designs are a personal way of looking at the world and commenting on it.

Before becoming hopelessly hung up on whittling bottle-stoppers, the reader should know that the same amount of physical energy can produce a work of art. Using tools, even mastering their use, is not the only requirement of good design. The other half of the coin is to educate your eyes for design. Become a noticer; a noticer of shapes, absence of shape, rhythm, and texture. Look around you! It's possible that only a thin hair-line separates a potential Henry Moore from a whittler. Both may be equally skilled in using their tools, but the one may not be using his eyes to pursue a design. This book, then, wants to make you look!

But if you're looking for a rulebook, I'm sorry, this isn't it. At times my statements may not sound dogmatic enough for your ears. If this happens, then I've succeeded. I can't give you rules. I can make suggestions, but you'll just have to find most things out for yourself by getting off the printed page and into your studio. I can shout loudly that tools must be sharp, but I cannot insist that there is only *one* way to hold a chisel, *one* way to make a cut, or *one* way to finish a completed design. For every hard-and-fast rule laid down in a loud voice, there is someone to come along and break the rule proving that the rule, to everyone's chagrin, was a myth.

Although common sense and curiosity are silent, they are rib-sticking truths to consider in every phase of wood design. A book cannot perform the work or move the hands of its reader. *You* must get off the page and perform for yourself. You must be willing to experiment. Don't be ashamed to goof. How else can you learn? A mistake is an excellent professor. Trial and error produce a far greater mental impact than words. Let your common sense and curiosity run free.

Wood is an art medium

The word *hobby*, when used in the sense of doodling, has a nasty connotation when applied to an art medium. Please, please don't think of doodling, or dabbling in wood. Pursuing wood design is a serious undertaking and the fire only ignites the imagination when one becomes totally involved. If you must have a doodling pastime, then try collecting stamps, chasing butterflies, or raising African violets. Wood designing is enough of a challenge in itself without being mentally shelved as a front porch, rocking chair pastime.

Wood design is an art medium; it's an opportunity to pour something out from within, to discover things about yourself, to give visual reality to an idea, a feeling, or a mood where mind, heart, and hands work in harmony. A wood designer will reach a feeling of intimacy with his material. Wood can be looked at, felt, and smelled. Some consider wood merely a substance, a dead matter for building; others feel it has a living quality which can be projected through the design. Whichever way you feel, wood rests with art.

Wood is not a plastic medium

You should know that wood is not a plastic medium: wood is rigid like stone. If you've got the urge to squeeze it like clay, mold it with your hands, or bang it into shape with a hammer, you'll find it just cannot be done. The process of creating a wood design (except with assembling parts into a construction, bending, and lamination) is a process of cutting away excess wood. Wood lacks

the spontaneity of a more plastic medium; it's not instantaneous. Because it's not malleable, design in wood holds an exciting challenge.

What about selling your designs?

If wood as a means of expression does capture you, then you'd do well to think about some of the positive and negative aspects of selling.

If the sole attraction to wood is making money (heaven forbid), I quickly suggest that you run right out and try a legitimate job like plumbing or selling used cars. Since objects in wood are produced by hand, labor hours are often astronomical.

If you sell, then stick with original designs, rather than "assembly line art," in which you produce the same design over and over. Keep away from converting labor hours into a dollar value. It doesn't work! All you'll come up with is a headache, and an involved plan for shortcuts. Accept the fact that you don't work by the hour. Just because you've come up with a fine design, don't let that shop keeper talk you into reproducing two dozen of them, exclusively for him, providing you deliver by next Thursday. Don't listen to him. "Assembly line art" is the death end to creativity and individual growth. Stick with original designs. Sell them if you can, and charge plenty. You're worth it!

Selling, on the positive side, helps you recoup an investment in tools, and provides an unspoken endorsement that your design is successful in the eyes of others. This helps the ego. Then, too, it gives you a chance to clean off those design-cluttered shelves, unhang those overhung walls, and

begin a period of new vitality. Without some outlet, the juices of a prolific designer can often turn sour. It's like writing 733 completed short stories without a single sale. The only recipient of your effort is a dark, silent desk drawer. Sooner or later a person can sink under the weight of his own ever-present effort.

Lists in this book

In the back of the book, I have included a list of museums across the country that house extensive collections of objects in wood. This list is offered as a source for stimulating ideas, should you sneak a spare weekend to indulge. I urge you to look at finished pieces first person. I have also included a list of suppliers: firms that supply tools, wood, and illustrated catalogs for reference. Then there is a bibliography, a listing of recommended books for further reading.

Summary

The gentle theme of the book, then, urges you to search for original freedom in wood design. In his poem, reprinted in part at the front of this book, Mr. Kazantzakis infers that without freedom—freedom to discover one's own ideas—there is little value in accumulating anything: wealth, material possessions, or even a nest filled with grandchildren. He would prefer the craftsman lay down his tools to search first for freedom. Artistic freedom is the essence of wood design. Tools directed by a mimeograph mind speak only an echo. And an echo sings only an empty song.

Nativity by the author. Tallest figure 16″ high; Pine. Carved in the round with an X-Acto knife, stained, and finished with three coats of satin finish varnish. Photo by Dave Congalton.

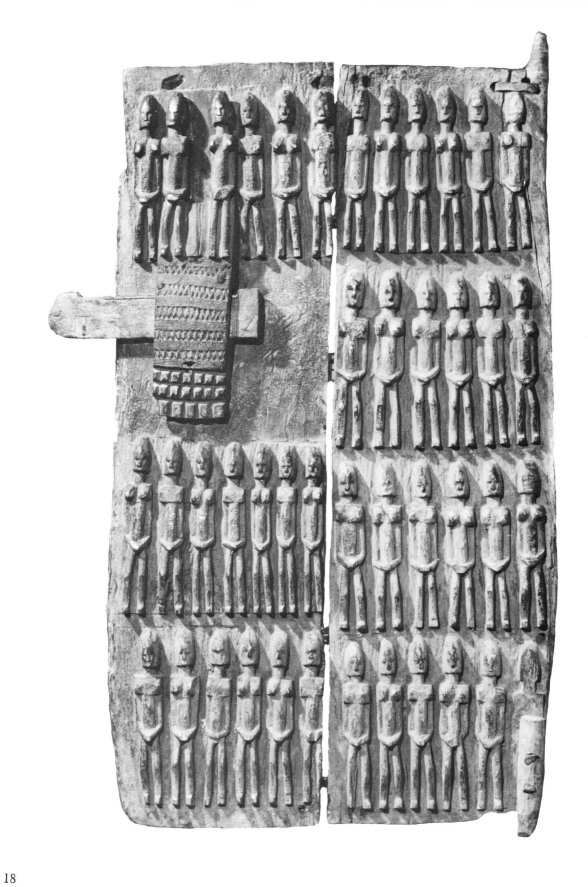

1 / The Studio

The first step in wood design is to develop an off-limits place to work; a private refuge from the rest of the house. If you try to improvise studio space by bobbing between lines of dripping laundry in the basement, or by producing between-meal "kitchen table art," you'll strangle the creative spirit before it even begins to move. Working in an inefficient atmosphere can be likened to trying to whittle a hunk of super hard black walnut with a broken razor-blade; perspiration and a second dose of aspirins are the only end results. The need for studio space then is a *must*, otherwise you'll be mentally—if not physically—fighting your atmosphere, your tools, and your ability to exercise those tools.

There are no absolutes in setting up a studio since there are no absolutes in people, their size, shape, working habits, or the space available to them. Privacy, a maximum of space, adequate light, and close proximity to electrical outlets are primary concerns.

If you have children, privacy is essential. Children can upset the equilibrium of a studio in less time than it takes to ruffle their posteriors for doing it. A maximum of space, preferably a room of your own, or at least a liberal corner (especially if you intend working on large items) is necessary. If you plan to work with machine electrical tools, your space requirements will be even greater. A 150 watt bulb, or its equivalent, will handle the lighting. High-intensity lamps are excellent for close work, especially if they are mounted on a flexible neck so you can spotlight them. It's important that the source of light comes from overhead, or from in front of the work. If light originates from behind you, it will leave your hands and your work in your body shadow. It's essential that you work near an electrical outlet if you plan to use electrical tools.

Wood is a clean medium. Chips and sawdust can be swept up or vacuumed. Incidentally, I suggest you plan to save your wood chips and sawdust. Chips make an excellent absorbent for oil stains on the garage floor, a quick kindling for a fireplace,

Granary door Mali: Dogon. 36½" high; wood. This functional door, carved in relief, gains rhythm through the repetition of design motif. Photo courtesy The Museum of Primitive Art.

Figure 1 *Workbench pushed tightly against corner of room for added stability. Swivel bench vice illustrated at left; woodworking vice on right.*

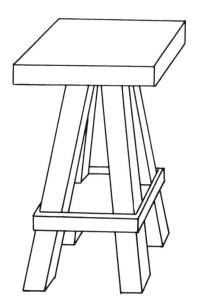

Figure 2 *Heavy duty modeling stand used in gaining easy access to all sides of sculpture.*

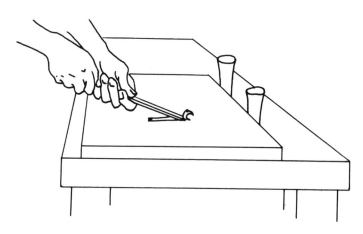

Figure 3 *Two bench stop pegs in use. Pegs fit tightly into holes drilled through bench work surface.*

and a practical animal bedding that absorbs both odor and moisture. You can also mix sawdust with glue for a wood filler.

The workbench

A workbench, above all, must be heavy. A flimsy bench will sag and slide under the constant impact of mallet on chisel. The bench should be constructed from thick lumber, the thicker the better. At least two-inch planks should be used for the work surface, and 4″ x 4″ corner posts for the legs. If you cannot locate heavy lumber, then be sure to anchor the bench to the floor. If the floor is made out of wood, the bench can be anchored with L–shaped angle irons screwed both to the legs and to the floor. If the bench rests on cement, you can add weight to the bench by constructing a low shelf under the work surface and stacking the shelf with cement blocks or heavy rocks. For another means of support you can shove the bench up against a corner location where the support of two walls will prevent it from moving. Begin with a solid, well anchored bench so you won't have to chase around the studio after it.

Use your own body build as a guide to the height of the bench work surface. Generally speaking, about hip height is comfortable. The length and width of the bench will depend upon the space you can spare. A bench twenty inches wide and four to five feet long will work for most projects. The bench doesn't have to be elegant. The frills or optional extras one might add to the bench are unrelated to the designer's skill in producing an interesting piece. If you're on a tight budget, four old barn timbers sawed for legs, and two heavy planks for the top will do the trick. Be certain your bench doesn't have a facing board across the front edge of the work surface. A facing board gets in the way when attaching clamps to the bench. Figure 1 suggests a very suitable workbench arrangement.

Stool

When hand work does not need the leverage of a standing position, a stool—adjusted to the comfort of the bench work surface—will provide a welcome addition to the studio. A kitchen step-stool is a good height, or you might even cut off the back from an outgrown highchair. If money's no problem, draftsmen's stools, ranging in height from 18 to 30 inches, are available through art supply dealers.

Hand tool storage

A drawer under the workbench is one solution for tool storage, but I prefer inexpensive clips fastened to the wall above the bench. This arrangement is illustrated in Figure 1. It provides quick access, a minimum of hunting, and keeps the tools from becoming scratched. Tools can pile up in a drawer, and it's not impossible to bury them under chips and debris that can, and will drop into an open drawer. Wall clips cost only a few cents each and provide a snug grip on handles. Another storage idea is to hang a piece of Masonite pegboard, equipped with pegboard tool hangers, above the bench. Masonite and pegboard tool hangers are available at lumber stores everywhere. Still a fourth solution is to wrap the tools in a cloth made with separate compartments for each tool.

It's important to protect hand tools from humidity. If the room is moist—a damp basement in summer for example—excess moisture may cause rust on the tool shafts. If rust appears, you should either remove the tools from the room, wrap them in cloth, or store them in a covered tool box. If tools go unused for long periods, rub them lightly along the shaft with an oily rag. This insulates the tools from rust. (Chapter 2 details the steps involved in sharpening tools.)

The vice and modeling stand

A vice is used to hold the project firmly in place while it's being worked on. There are two types of vices: the swivel bench vice, and the woodworking vice (both types are illustrated in Figure 1). These vices are attached to the bench with heavy lag bolts. Every studio should include at least one of these two vices. The swivel bench vice rotates on a central pivot allowing convenient access to all sides of the project. The woodworking vice doesn't pivot. It's simply a strong, and broad holding device. When buying a vice, inquire about the maximum opening of the vice jaw. A small jaw cannot hold a large project. You'll want to be sure your vice will hold the size you intend tackling. If the vice has metal jaws, a thin piece of wood, cork, or leather should be inserted between the jaw edge and the wood to act as a buffer. This buffer will prevent the metal jaws from denting or branding the wood.

A free-standing modeling stand (Figure 2) is an excellent addition to the studio when you want to get at all sides of your project, to walk around and study it. The swivel bench vice can perform the functions of a modeling stand for projects that will fit within the maximum jaw opening. On larger items, the modeling stand can solve the problem of access: you'll be able to reach the project without stretching your neck. Like the workbench, a modeling stand can be homemade. Be sure that it is well anchored and free of a work surface facing board. Whether you use a swivel bench vice, a woodworking vice, or a modeling stand is a matter of taste and budget. Whichever you use, be sure the project is held tight while you work on it. Chapter 2 will explain the use of clamps and how to anchor the project to the bench work surface.

Additional bench features

A length of old carpet, tacked to the work surface of the bench, will provide a cushion against which to work and will protect your project from unplanned denting. A bench stop, or series of stops, will give you something firm to shove against when you're using a chisel or gouge in a forward thrust. Stops are made by drilling holes through the work surface of the bench and inserting snug wooden plugs into the holes. Plugs can be whittled from scrap wood. The number of plugs used will depend upon the width of your design and on how much pressure you exert against them. Use your own judgment. Stability is what you're after. The plugs should extend above the work surface about three inches, and should be cushioned to eliminate denting. Figure 3 illustrates how a bench stop plug is used.

Gallery

I think it's a good beginning to reserve some space in your studio for a gallery: a place to display your completed work. A series of weathered barn boards against a white wall can serve as handsome shelf space. Wall hangings against the same white wall will compliment your designs. The presence of your own work will keep you visually concerned with its design, how the object invades the space around it, and what you can do to display it against the most complimentary background. Then too, a gallery can provide a stimulant to further ideas. A gallery also adds a professional atmosphere. For the cook, the dining room, where everything is planned, orderly, and attractive is the most complimentary atmosphere to serve a skillful menu. This cook would shudder at the thought of entertaining guests at her messy sink. Likewise, a clutter of tools, wood chips, and paint pans does little to compliment a completed wood design.

Christ by Maria (Maria Martins), 1941. 7'10½" high; Jacaranda wood. A close-up of the rough gouge-textured surface. Collection, The Museum of Modern Art, New York, gift of Nelson A. Rockefeller.

Two partridges by Russ Burr. (above) Mounted on driftwood and painted. Photo by Einars J. Mengis; courtesy Shelburne Museum, Inc.

Pantocrator by Mike Nevelson. (right) 8′ high. (Silvermine Award, 1965) Vertical strips of laminated Pine create strength of line through lamination and grain figure. Photo courtesy of the artist.

2 / Tools

Given two hands and practice, anyone can learn to use tools. A great number of tools, both hand and machine, are available for wood design; this chapter will introduce many of them.

Buying your first tools

Please don't run out and buy a kit of hand tools—or one of everything that meets the eye. Tools should be purchased like a hat. You can wear only one hat at a time, and likewise you can use only one tool at a time. Be fussy! Selection is important. Don't buy a tool until you need it. Experiment with what you have and then move ahead with mellowed growth. Only in this way can you master your tools instead of becoming their victim.

Wood design does not require a heavy investment in tools. Listed below is a beginning selection of hand tools available for under $50.00. As practice develops skill, and as the lock on your imagination gains freedom, you may want to increase your purchases in one of several directions. The hand tools listed will keep you busy experimenting for a long time, and they can be used to render a wide variety of design techniques. These tools are numbered by the English numbering system.

Gouges Number 5 (⅝ inch straight gouge). Number 3 (1 inch straight gouge). Number 7 (⅜ inch straight gouge).

Parting Tool (Optional) Number 39 (½ inch straight parting tool).

Chisel Number 1 (½ inch straight firmer chisel).

Knives Number 75. X-Acto Carving Chest.

Mallet One medium weight lignumvitae mallet.

Stones One Arkansas bench stone (or India oilstone), fine grade. One India gouge slip stone, fine grade. One tapered oilstone, fine grade.

Rasps One half-round 8 inch rasp, fine cut. One half-round 8 inch rasp, coarse cut.

Oil One small can of household oil.

Monad by Jane Teller, 1964. 5½′ high; Cherry and Hemlock. To cut her pieces, the artist uses a combination of a large band saw and a portable Sawzall power hack saw. This piece is naturally finished with Val Oil. Photo by R. Knight; courtesy of the artist.

Quality in tools

There is no substitute for high quality tools, especially hand tools where the cutting edge is subjected to continual resharpening. The ease with which you're able to execute your design depends upon that cutting edge. If the quality of the tool is such that it can hold its cutting edge, withstand normal pressure, and submit to resharpening, then you have a high quality tool.

Cut-rate tools are available at discount stores everywhere. Beware of bargain tools! A tool is an investment in your ability to perform with it.

Imported tools with tempered steel or hollow ground shafts are generally the best investment. Another safe guide are tools advertised for the professional. Professional tools are usually high in quality. A poorly designed tool, made of inexpensive material, is of little value if the shaft breaks under pressure. It may have been a bargain, but if the shaft of the tool snaps off, leaving the broken end imbedded in your design, the tears you shed will not be named economy.

The use of tools

This text will not blow windy paragraphs on the use of tools. I can tell you what a specific tool is used for and how it works, but you must experiment with it yourself to really get to know it well. My words cannot provide your practice. Practice comes only from doing. Confidence comes first; proficiency second. In the beginning, it's necessary to experiment; take a chunk of wood and doodle. And then take another. Hack away at them! Go ahead! Make mistakes! Find out what your tools will do; what they cannot do. My words might well drift past you, but your own trial and error will stick hard; "a rib stickin' peanut-butter lesson," as a friend of mine once said. You must gain an intimacy with your tools. This only comes from using them.

Although many tools overlap in their function—it's possible to make the same cut with a variety of tools—one tool in particular may be designed specifically to make that cut easier and cleaner. For example, a jackknife will cut a V groove, but so will a parting tool. A jackknife requires twice the effort—two strokes, instead of one—and even at that the cut will still probably turn out ragged on the edges. The parting tool is designed to make the same V groove smoothly, with a minimum risk to control. The staid Down East whittler may stick by his jackknife for the V groove, but that doesn't make it the rule. All he's really proving is that he's stubborn. Tools, then, are designed for efficiency; efficiency in labor and ease of result. If you want to create a particular effect, and there's a tool specifically designed to render that effect, then why not use that tool instead of working as though you were born with two left hands? It's like trying to build a house using only a jackknife and a rock; the knife for a saw, and the rock for a hammer. It's possible, but what do you really prove?

Tools may be grouped according to function. *Cutting tools* include knives, chisels, gouges, the parting tool, the veiner, the adz, the drawknife, and disposable blade tools. *Abrasive tools* include rasps, rifflers, and sharpening tools. *Machine tools* include the jigsaw, the bandsaw, the motor-tool, the sabre saw, power hacksaw, and power sanding tools. *Holding tools* include vices and clamps. In addition to these tools, there are a few miscellaneous items including brushes, sandpaper, steel wool, and protective devices. These additions are equally a part of wood design. Now I'll describe each group individually.

The cutting tool and its use

A cutting tool is used to remove wood. It may be used to reduce a piece of wood to a finished design—as in the case of sculpture—or it may be used to cut surface decoration into the wood—as in the case of chip carving and incised work. In either case, the tool is removing wood. Cutting tools include knives, chisels, gouges, the parting tool, the veiner, the drawknife, and the carver's adz.

Chelsea reach II by Gabriel Kohn, 1960-61.
24½″ x 52½″; laminated wood construction.
Dowel pin lamination used to create wood volume.
Photo courtesy Marlborough-Gerson Gallery.

Marzipan mold, undated. (above) 15″ x 25½″; Mahogany. Symmetrical balance with Washington closed by a circle and balanced on both sides by the repetition of an eagle. Photo by Einars J. Mengis; courtesy Shelburne Museum, Inc.

Eagle, nineteenth century. (right) 33½″ high. This symbol of America stands proud and dignified because the wings have been tucked close to the body, creating one vertical plane. Photo by Einars J. Mengis; courtesy Shelburne Museum, Inc.

In order not to get ahead of ourselves, and before describing each of the cutting tools, I should explain the handling of a tool: how to hold a cutting tool; some of the elements of wood grain; the principles involved in making the cut. Once over this hurdle, the reader should be able to leap in, hands first, to handle each of the tools in order of appearance.

How to hold the cutting tool

No two people are alike. The cutting tool should be held the way it feels the most comfortable. Some suggestions follow; these are not meant to be rigid rules. The methods as described do work for me. If you discover something better, then please stick with it.

The knife should be held in the hand that exercises the most strength and control. If you're right handed, you'll want to hold the knife in your right hand. One way of holding the knife is to place the handle in the palm of your hand with the blade projecting from the thumb end. The cutting edge of the blade can then either be stroked toward the body—as in peeling potatoes—or away from the body—as in striking a wooden match against its box. When the knife is used for outlining or chip carving (see Chapter 5 for techniques on chip carving), it is held like a pencil, with the index finger applying a downward pressure on the back of the blade.

The chisel, gouge, veiner, and parting tool are held in a manner opposite from that of the knife. If you're right handed, you'll want to hold the chisel, gouge, veiner, and parting tool in your *left* hand and the mallet with your *right* hand, as shown in Figure 4. When using one of these tools without a mallet, you should cradle the rounded end of the tool handle in the palm of your right hand. In this position, the right hand acts as the mallet in providing the downward pressure for the cutting edge of the tool. The left hand is then either placed above or below the shaft of the tool, depending on the most comfortable position for

you. Figure 5 illustrates the left hand *above*; Figure 6 illustrates the left hand *below* the shaft.

Some people will find it more comfortable to place the left hand under the shaft, as shown in Figure 6, in order to gain a *lifting* pressure on the cutting edge. Others will prefer to place the left hand above the shaft to gain a *downward* pressure, as in Figure 5. Basically, the right hand is producing a forward thrust of the cutting edge; the left hand then holds the tool and equalizes that forward thrust by keeping the force and direction of the thrust under control. A pushing and pulling of the tool takes place at the same time to keep the direction of the cutting edge under control.

Experiment for yourself in holding the cutting tool. Try it both ways, and select whichever position you find comfortable. The only loud rule when holding a cutting tool is to keep your hands away from in front of the blade. It's sharp!

Finding the wood grain

All wood has grain. Some grains are more prominent than others. Grain is formed by new layers of wood; one new layer builds upon another. As the tree grows, each new layer of wood forms a concentric ring around a common core. The fibers of grain run the length of the trunk from base to top or, in other words, they run from the ground level up to the branches, or crown of the tree. The distance between two given fibers is not always the same. It varies in random widths. For example, a limb might start its life between two given fibers and cause the fibers to spread, or bulge out to accommodate the sprouting limb. You can identify the grain by the light pattern of lines, or fibers, within the wood substance. This pattern of lines has both length and variable depth.

The direction of grain varies just as the distance between fibers varies. Direction will vary according to the circumference of the trunk at both the base and crown, and according to whether a given piece of wood was sawed with the grain, against the grain, or sawed at an angle. Since the blade of the

Figure 4 Holding the cutting tool when used with a mallet. Left thumb is placed along tool handle for added stability. Mallet is struck against tool handle in short jabs with pivot at the elbow.

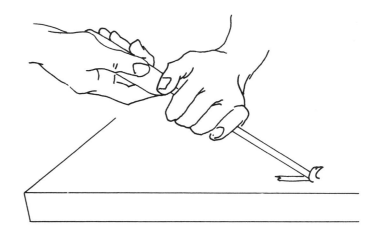

Figure 5 Holding the cutting tool without a mallet; the left hand is placed above the shaft to gain a downward equalizing pressure on the blade.

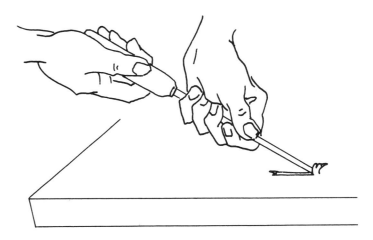

Figure 6 Holding the cutting tool without a mallet (*a second position*); the left hand is placed below the shaft to gain an upward equalizing pressure on the blade.

33

Untitled by Richard Baringer. Made of bent plywood with metal feet, sections are 18″ x 18″ and pinned together at the top and bottom. Mr. Baringer attempts to create a three dimensional painting by pulling it off the canvas and giving it sculptural form through bent plywood. Photo courtesy Dwan Gallery.

cutting tool violates the surface of wood, and therefore must sever the grain or wood fiber, the direction of grain *must* be determined before making the cut.

How to determine the direction of grain

To determine the direction of the grain, lay the block of wood on a flat surface up against something solid, or hold it firmly in a vice. (The grain, again, is identified by that series of random lines running within the wood substance.) Make a shallow cut in one direction along the grain. If the tool bites into the wood you are going *against* the grain. If the tool tends to rise back to the surface you are going *with* the grain.

Figure 7 illustrates what happens when the tool digs in the wrong direction: *against* the grain. The wood fibers break unevenly and the tool continues to dig deeper into the wood. The tool, in Figure 7, is following between the layers of wood fiber and is being drawn downward by the direction of grain. What happens is similar to a run in a woman's stocking. When the stocking fiber is snagged, the run leaps out of control. It follows the weave and there is nothing to prevent it from a quick trip to the toe. A cut *against* the grain will follow the "weave" of the wood fiber deeper into the wood.

Figure 8 illustrates the *correct* cut where the cut is made *with* the grain. In this illustration, the tool is being forced back to the surface by the direction of grain; the direction of grain is producing a built-in snag resister. The cutting edge of the tool rises with the grain as the pressure on the handle slacks off. A cut *with* the grain actually severs the wood fiber, rather than breaking it unevenly as happened in Figure 7. The result is a clean, free chip. If the tool begins to dig in, simply turn the block around or go at it from the other end.

Each piece of wood has a unique grain characteristic. You *must* find the direction of grain for each new piece of wood before you work on it. You'll avoid much aggravation by doing so.

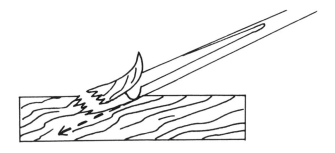

Figure 7 *This shows a slice cut made* against *the grain. The gouge blade digs into the wood, causing the wood fibers to break unevenly.*

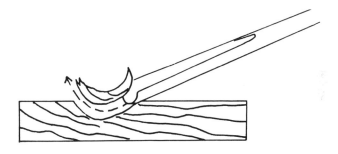

Figure 8 *The correct slice cut made* with *the grain will cause the cutting edge of the tool to rise back to the surface, leaving a clean chip.*

Making the cut

A cut is made to remove wood or to engrave surface decoration. There are two basic cuts: a stop cut and a slice cut.

Making the stop cut. A stop cut functions like nail polish applied to the run in a woman's stocking. Just as the nail polish stops the run in the stocking, the stop cut stops the run on the grain. If you want to remove a wedge or chip of wood of limited length, then you would *first* make a stop cut at that point where the wedge will end. The stop cut therefore limits, or *stops* the length of the over-all wedge while producing an even, clean end to the wedge. If you don't use a stop cut, there would be no way of precisely controlling the length of the over-all wedge, or chip. A precise design without stop cuts would be feathered into visual ambiguity. The stop cut is made *against* the grain, as in Figure 9 where a chisel is shown cutting the fibers across the grain. A chisel is usually used to make a stop cut, unless it happens to be a situation where you are using a knife to make a chisel stroke. As in Figure 9, the stop cut is executed by inserting the cutting edge of the chisel straight into the wood to whatever depth is desired of the wedge. The straight edge of the chisel leaves a clean virtical side to the cut, while the beveled edge of the chisel is turned toward the inside of the wedge.

Making the slice cut. The slice cut is a slice into the wood substance to remove wood. It can be executed alone or combined with a stop cut. Figure 8 illustrates a slice cut used alone. Figure 10 illustrates the same slice cut when used in combination with a stop cut to complete a wedge. The slice cut in both figures is made with a gouge. A slice cut may also be made with a knife, a parting tool, or a veiner. Unlike the stop cut, the slice cut runs *with* the lines of wood fiber and is made *with* the grain, as in Figure 8, so the cutting edge of the tool will rise back to the surface. A variety of effects can be rendered when using the slice cut alone, or when combining it with a stop cut. For example, in sculpture, when reducing a mass of wood to a finished form, a slice cut is used alone. In chip carving, or in outlining for a relief carving, a slice cut is combined with a stop cut to make a V– or L–shaped groove. The best thing to do is to experiment yourself. Try making a V groove with two opposing stop cuts, and then with one stop cut and one long slice cut. And then try other combinations. See how many you can come up with.

The knife

An effective and original wood design can be completed with only a knife. A broad rule is that a knife generally is restricted in use to designs small enough to hold in the hand, as for example, small pieces of sculpture under 18 inches in height. The

knife is also used for chip carving: a special knife is available for that purpose. Once the size of the design exceeds your grasp, you'll have to graduate to tools that require both hands; one hand to hold the tool, and the other as either the source of pressure upon the tool, or to hold the mallet that produces the pressure.

A variety of knives is available for work in wood design. Many people prefer using an ordinary jackknife because of the extra weight, the slender taper of the blade, and the added length of cutting edge. At the beginning of this chapter an initial purchase of a number 75, X-Acto Carving Chest was suggested. This chest will provide several handles, and a variety of inexpensive knife blades.

Four other knives are illustrated in Figures 11, 12, 13, and 14. Figure 11 illustrates a *chip carving knife* used when making surface decoration. To use this knife, pressure is applied in a downward motion toward the *skew*, or slanted cutting edge of the blade. Figure 12 is another *chip carving knife* where the action is either one of pressing down on the back of the blade with the index finger, or of a pulling stroke toward the body with the handle. Figure 13 is a *fine carving knife* with a thin tapered cutting edge for shallow strokes, or for getting at hard-to-reach places. Figure 14 is a *whittling knife* where, like the jackknife, the stroke is either toward you, or away from you. All of these knives are inexpensive.

The chisel

A wood carving chisel can be identified by its straight cutting edge. It differs from a carpenter's chisel in that it has a longer bevel, or slant on the cutting edge. The straight cutting edge makes it a tool for outlining, and for executing stop cuts. The flat side provides a smooth edge to the outline while the beveled surface pushes a wedge. The chisel is used extensively when outlining on a relief and incised design.

There are two types of chisels: the skew chisel and the straight chisel. Figure 15 illustrates a skew

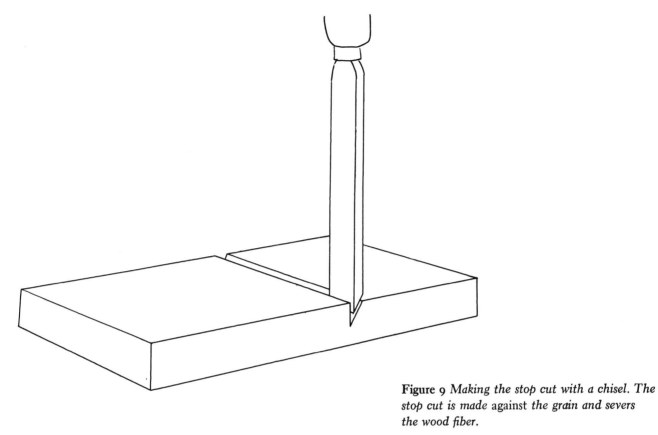

Figure 9 *Making the stop cut with a chisel. The stop cut is made against the grain and severs the wood fiber.*

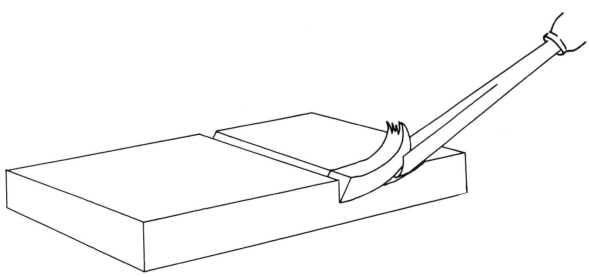

Figure 10 *Making a slice cut with a gouge. The slice cut is made with the grain resulting in a clean, even chip.*

Nudesville by William King, 1963. (left) 32¾″ high; Mahogany. One black stocking is the means by which Mr. King establishes asymmetrical balance on this figure that would otherwise seem to want to put its foot down. Photo by John F. Waggaman; courtesy Terry Dintenfass Gallery.

Sweetie by William King, 1963. (right) 26″ high; Mahogany. Simplicity and a kinship with folk vision seem to shout from this piece. Compare it with Anne Arnold's *Geoffrey* on page 119. By eliminating detail (hands, feet, dress pattern), Mr. King strengthens the visual impact. The viewer is not called upon to inspect this piece minutely before catching its strength. Photo by John F. Waggaman; courtesy Terry Dintenfass Gallery. Collection, Mr. and Mrs. Robert M. Benjamin.

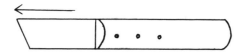

Figure 11 *A chip carving knife used with a downward pressure directed toward the angled cutting edge of the tool. (Arrow indicates direction of pressure.)*

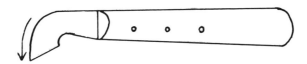

Figure 12 *A chip carving knife where downward pressure is applied to the back of the blade between the handle and the curve. Pressure is applied with the index finger. (Arrow indicates direction of pressure.)*

Figure 13 *A fine carving knife, used for shallow strokes. (Arrow indicates direction of pressure.)*

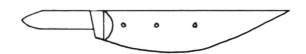

Figure 14 *A whittling knife, used in the same manner as a jackknife with the stroke away from the body or toward the body, depending upon whichever is the most comfortable.*

Figure 15 *A skew chisel used for making stop cuts and outlining; also used in chip carving.*

chisel with its angled cutting edge. It is an outlining tool. The straight chisel, Figure 16, is used to make a stop cut, and for outlining. A chisel is normally used with a mallet, although it can be used with hand pressure on soft woods. Chisels are sold by width of cutting edge. They run in width from ⅛ inch to 1 inch; the wider the blade, the wider the cut.

The gouge

A gouge has a curved cutting edge in the shape of a broad U. It's used to make a slice cut and to remove wood: a cut similar to a scoop with gently tapered sides. Figures 17, 18, and 19 illustrate three types of gouges: the straight gouge, the spoon gouge, and the long bent gouge. A gouge is normally used with a mallet, although like the chisel, it can be used with only hand pressure on soft wood. While the gouge produces a U cut, the chisel, if used in the same way, produces a flat cut with ragged, right angled edges. Gouges vary in width from ⅛ inch to 1 inch; the broader the U, the larger the scoop.

The parting tool

A parting tool has a V–shaped shaft and cutting edge, and is used for outlining and for cutting a V groove. It can be used for texture strokes, surface decoration, and chip carving. Figure 20 illustrates a parting tool. A parting tool can be used with or without a mallet, depending upon which is easier for a given piece of wood. Several widths are available from ⅛ inch and larger; each producing a broader and deeper V as the size increases.

The veiner

A veiner has a tight, shallow U–shaped shaft and cutting edge. It produces a shallow *vein* in the wood surface (smaller than the scoop of a gouge), and is used in outlining, and creating shallow texture strokes on surface decoration. Figure 21 illustrates the veiner.

The carver's adz

A carver's adz is shaped something like an ordinary hammer. Figure 22 illustrates the carver's adz. Instead of the claw tip found on a hammer, there is a gouge on one side, and a heavy chisel bit on the opposite side. A carver's adz is used on large pieces where a great deal of wood must be removed before the fine carving is begun. The adz is swung in a manner similar to a hammer, only in short, hard jabs with the pivot of the swing at the elbow, rather than at the wrist.

The drawknife

The drawknife looks like a butcher's knife, except that it has curved wooden handles on both ends. Figure 23 illustrates the drawknife. The drawknife is used for heavy work when there is a lot of excess wood to be removed; similar in use to the carver's adz. The drawknife is pulled toward the body; both hands are gripped firmly on the handles to balance an even cut, and to control depth. Like the adz, and on large designs, the drawknife produces a hand-hewn mark, excellent for texture.

The mallet

Although the mallet is not a cutting tool, it belongs with the cutting tools because it is used with the cutting tool; it produces the force that drives the cutting tool into the wood. Figure 24 illustrates a mallet. Mallets are made out of extremely hard wood, usually lignumvitae, an unusually heavy wood of the bean-caper family. Mallets are sold by weight. Heavier mallets are used with deeper cuts, especially wide and deep-scooped gouges. The side of a mallet is struck against the top of the tool (see Figure 4). It is swung like the adz with the pivot at the elbow.

Disposable blade tools

A disposable blade tool is a two-part tool with a handle and a variety of interchangeable, disposable

Figure 16 *A straight chisel used in making stop cuts and in outlining.*

Figure 17 *A straight gouge.*

Figure 18 *A spoon gouge*

Figure 19 *A long bent gouge.*

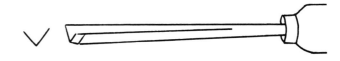

Figure 20 *A parting tool, used for making V cuts.*

Figure 21 *A veiner used in making shallow outline and texture strokes.*

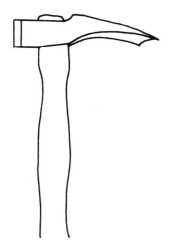

Figure 22 *A carver's adz, with gouge and chisel bit on either side.*

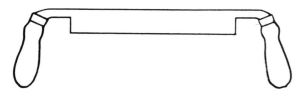

Figure 23 *A drawknife held with both hands and pulled toward the body.*

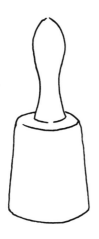

Figure 24 *A medium weight lignumvitae mallet.*

blades. It's an excellent tool for chip carving, and for carving soft wood designs small enough to hold in the hand. The disposable blade tool is not effective on large pieces (that is, pieces larger than hand size), and it's only mediocre on hard wood. Its value lies with soft wood.

The *X-Acto Company* manufactures an excellent disposable blade tool. The handles—which come in three sizes—unscrew for the insertion of blades. The blades are precision sharp. Available blades include knife blades, chisel blades, gouges, and routers. Blades are so inexpensive that when a blade gets dull it can be discarded. Figure 25 illustrates an inexpensive selection of disposable blade tools. I find it a tool hard to be without.

Hand saws

If you don't plan to use electrical machine tools, then I suggest you invest in a carpenter's crosscut saw and a coping saw. The crosscut saw will quickly dispose of excess wood when you want to reduce a piece of sculpture to a silhouette; the coping saw, because of its thin blade, can be used to remove excess wood on fussy curves and pierced openings.

Abrasive tools

The next group of tools is the abrasives. An abrasive tool is used to smooth and to remove wood. Abrasive tools include the rasp, the riffler, the file, sandpaper, and steel wool.

The wood rasp

A wood rasp is used for removing wood and for smoothing. The blade or cutting shaft of a wood rasp is made of either a fine, medium, or coarse metallic surface. A coarse rasp is used for removing wood; it is an excellent sculpting tool. A fine rasp is used for smoothing the wood. The rasp is held in the same manner as a carpenter's plane—with one hand on the handle, and the other hand ahead

—applying the downward pressure in a long, even stroke. The rasp is stroked at a diagonal to the wood grain. Figure 26 illustrates a wood rasp. Rasps are often sold without handles. Handles are available separately, and are very inexpensive.

The riffler file

A riffler file has a medium to fine cutting surface, and is used to smooth, or clean out hard to reach places on fine work. It's curved and tapered on both ends so that it can be easily inserted into holes, or around corners. Rifflers are available in a wide variety of shapes and cutting surfaces. Needle files—another abrasive tool for fine work—are similar to rifflers, except that needle files have a straight shaft and are not as adaptable to poking around hard to reach corners. Figure 27 illustrates a riffler; Figure 28 a needle file. If you have an occasion to work on a piece with small holes, or with narrow grooves, like between fingers on a human hand, then one or both of these tools will come in handy. They're very inexpensive.

Sandpaper and steel wool

Sandpaper and steel wool are abrasives used for smoothing a finished piece. These items are sold in hardware stores everywhere by the grade, or weight of the cutting surface: fine, medium, and coarse. When using these items, be sure you don't overdo the coarseness of cutting surface or you'll leave scratch marks on the piece of wood. A hard-grained, coarse sandpaper rubbed across a piece of walnut will raise havoc with the surface. It would have been better, in that instance, to use a medium-to-fine grade of paper. You'll have to experiment for yourself. If, right off the bat, you tackle the task of sanding with the gusto of a robust washerwoman using a scrub board, you may scar the wood. Begin with gentleness until you've determined the proper grade of paper for the given piece of wood.

Sometimes, with certain types of wood, the

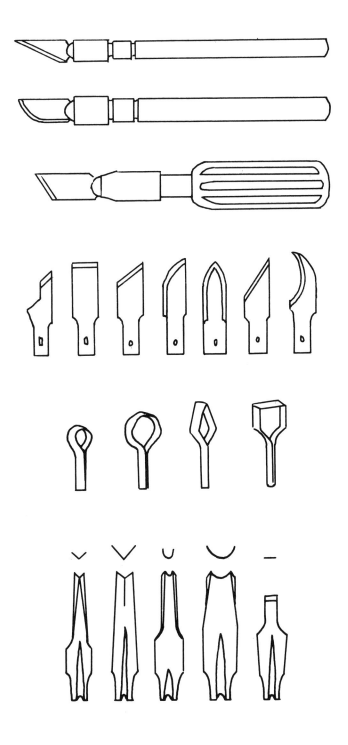

Figure 25 *An inexpensive selection of disposable blade X-Acto knives. Top row shows cutting knife blades, middle row shows four routers, and bottom row shows gouge and parting tool blades.*

grains on the sandpaper will fill with sawdust. When this happens, tap the paper against the edge of the bench. If this doesn't remove the sawdust, then lightly rub the cutting surface with a wire brush. A cloth or fiber backed sandpaper will give twice the wear.

Sharpening tools

Sharpening tools are abrasives; an abrasive, when used on hand tools, grinds or wears away a dull surface to expose a fresh, sharp surface. Stones, slips, the razor strop, and heavy leather are all sharpening abrasives used to sharpen hand tools. Each abrasive has its unique surface texture and hardness for wearing away or grinding on metal. A stone is an extremely hard abrasive, shaped in a cube. A slip is equally as hard as a stone, but is manufactured in specific shapes to cradle the curves and bevels on hand tools. The razor strop is a smooth and flexible leather abrasive used in finishing the final stages of sharpening. If a strop is not available, a piece of heavy leather—preferably horsehide—will serve the same purpose.

Sharpening stones and slips are sold by grade, ranging from coarse to fine, and they are used in the same progression. A very dull tool must first be worked on a coarse abrasive, and then worked in progression from medium to fine abrasive. The final abrasive—the leather strop—is the least coarse. Unless you break a piece out of your tool, you should be able to get along with medium to fine abrasives.

When sharpening a cutting edge, the tool moves on the abrasive rather than the abrasive being rubbed across the tool. Remember how a barber sharpens his razor? His leather strop is fastened firmly to the chair. He moves the razor back and forth along the strop. This is the same principle for stones, slips, and the strop. Keep your abrasive stationary and move the tool across it. Either hold it firmly in your hand or clamp it in the vice.

Stones and slips have natural pores. A drop or two of light household oil is used on both stones

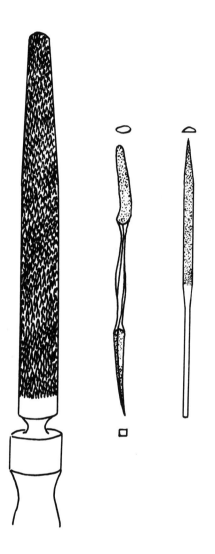

Figure 26 (left) A coarse wood rasp used as a sculpting tool in removing wood.

Figure 27 (center) A riffler, used in hard-to-reach places for smoothing.

Figure 28 (right) A needle file, used as a smoothing tool.

Eagle, nineteenth century. 2'6½" high with a 2'10¾"
wingspread; Pine. This piece was used as a public
building ornament. The fierce and menacing attitude
of the eagle is gained through the diagonal line of
the wing position, body, and claw. Photo by
Einars J. Mengis; courtesy Shelburne Museum, Inc.

45

Blanket chest, chip carved. 36″ long x 18″ wide x 39″ high; Pine construction, painted dark reddish-brown. The top eagle and the front scene are carved in relief and framed by chip carved borders. Photo by Einars J. Mengis; courtesy Shelburne Museum, Inc.

and slips to keep the pores from becoming clogged with the residue left from grinding away the metal. However, oil should *not* be used on a strop. Figure 29 illustrates a flat oilstone in a cube; Figure 30 illustrates a shaped gouge slip; Figure 31 illustrates a tapered oilstone.

It's important that you learn how to sharpen your own tools. Dull tools will quickly transform a pleasurable experience into a hair-tearing nightmare. Tool manufacturers have been kind (or lazy) enough to provide retail stores with unsharpened tools, so the business of sharpening will be your concern as soon as you take home your new tool. Both sides of the tool have to be sharpened. Most new tools have only been roughly ground on one side, necessitating an immediate exercise in sharpening.

How to sharpen a knife

Knives are sharpened first on a fine India oilstone, and then finished on a piece of heavy leather, or a strop (the leather and strop are identical in purpose). To sharpen a knife, first lay the blade on the oilstone, then raise the back edge of the knife slightly off the stone. Draw the cutting edge of the knife blade back and forth across the stone, first one side and then the other until a fine wire edge appears along the edge. See Figures 32 and 33. Remove this wire edge with the strop or the leather, using the same back and forth motion, being careful not to dig the blade into the leather. The longer the bevel on any cutting tool, the easier it will make a cut. One obvious exception is not to get so carried away with lengthening the bevel that the thickness of the blade is worn thin. If this happens, the cutting bevel may break off under pressure.

How to sharpen the chisel

Chisels are sharpened on a flat oilstone (Figure 29). The beveled edge is sharpened on the stone, and the straight edge is honed with a strop to

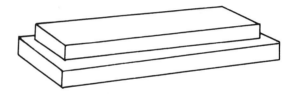

Figure 29 *An oilstone, used for sharpening knives and chisels.*

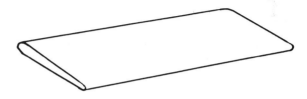

Figure 30 A *gouge slip, used in sharpening the outside edge of the gouge.*

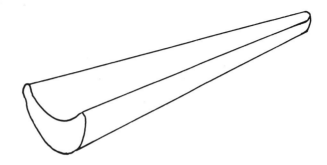

Figure 31 A *tapered oilstone with rounded edges for honing inside bevels.*

47

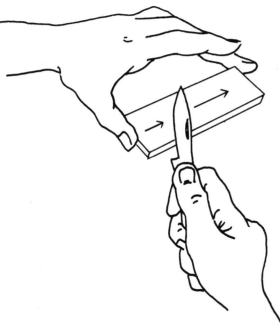

Figure 32 *Sharpening a knife; stroking the blade away from the body.*

Figure 33 *Sharpening a knife; stroking the blade toward the body.*

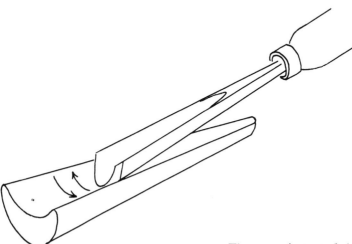

Figure 34 *A gouge being sharpened in a gouge slip. The cutting edge of the gouge is rocked back and forth in the cradle of the slip as indicated by arrows.*

remove the final wire edge. To sharpen a chisel, hold the bevel flat against the stone, draw the bevel along the full length of the stone, back and forth several times, until a wire edge appears. The wire edge is removed with the leather or strop in the same manner as with the knife. It's important to apply equal pressure to all points of the cutting edge so the edge will remain constant to avoid creating pits, or hollows. Occasionally check the bevel to make sure it remains flat, and if you're using more than one stone, remember to work from coarse, to medium, to fine. Before you put away your equipment, test the tool for sharpness on a piece of soft wood. The tool should cut evenly, not tear; it should "whistle" through the wood.

How to sharpen the parting tool

The two sides of the parting tool can be treated as chisels and sharpened separately, the same as the chisel. Be careful when you sharpen around the point of the V. This point is not supposed to be a sharp, exact point. Actually, it should be treated as a tiny gouge, blending gradually into the straight side edges of the parting tool. The inside of the parting tool is sharpened with the narrow rounded edge of the tapered oilstone illustrated in Figure 31; just enough of a bevel to remove the outside wire edge.

How to sharpen the gouge

A fine gouge slip is used to sharpen a gouge (unless the blade is all nicked up, in which case you'd have to resort to a coarse stone and work up to fine). A gouge slip is shaped to cradle the beveled cutting edge of the gouge as illustrated in Figure 34. Sharpen the gouge by placing the beveled cutting edge in the cradle of the stone, rocking the cutting edge fully back and forth from side to side, flat against the stone surface. It's important not to press harder in one spot than in another, and it's equally important to keep the handle of

the gouge always at the same angle away from the stone. The finished edge of the gouge is worked smooth on a strop. The inside cutting edge of the gouge can be given a gentle bevel by lightly rocking it against the broad rounded edge of the oilstone, as illustrated in Figure 31. Sharpen the veiner in the same manner as prescribed for the gouge.

Machine tools

Machine tools are electric tools. They include the jigsaw, the bandsaw, the motor-tool, the sabre saw, the power hacksaw, and electric sanding tools. There are other electrical tools that can be used for occasional work in wood, such as the bench saw, the joiner, and power drills, but this text will not cover these items.

There are two opposing schools of thought regarding the use of machine tools. One argument runs that machine tools have no part in the creation of a wood design. This argument holds that wood design *must* be entirely hand produced; that the use of machine tools is premeditated fraud, and destroys the esthetic worth of the design. The opposite argument holds that machine tools save endless hours of hand labor, and open new doors for design possibilities. This argument maintains that design is not dependent upon the technique used in reaching the finished piece; that design transcends the tool and either works or does not work independently of how it is achieved. There are outstanding professionals in each persuasion. I won't take sides, and perhaps this is the coward's out. I will say, however, that machine tools and contemporary techniques are much too important to be ignored in a text of this type. I leave the reader to carry the banner.

The jigsaw

Most of my comments on the jigsaw are negative. It's just too small a machine to be of much practical use in wood design. It can be used on a limited basis for cutting the profile on small pieces of sculpture. Figures 48 to 52 in Chapter 5 on techniques illustrates how the profile is cut. Perhaps the most positive comment on the jigsaw is to say that if you can afford one, add a few extra dollars to the pile and buy a bandsaw.

The bandsaw

A bandsaw will do the work of a jigsaw—and much more. It will save labor in reducing a piece of sculpture to a profile; it will get rid of excess wood in minutes, compared with hours of hacking with an adz or drawknife. A bandsaw is capable of comfortably handling wood up to four inches thick; a few workshop bandsaws will tackle pieces six inches thick. If you want to work larger than six inches, you'll have to locate an industrial bandsaw, mark the profile on the wood, and then carry the wood to wherever the saw is located. When buying a bandsaw, consider the length of the saw throat (the *throat* is that area behind the blade that allows room to pivot the wood). A shallow throat will handle only a short piece of wood.

The motor-tool

The motor-tool is an electric tool equipped with interchangeable blades: cutting blades, engraving bits, sanding tips, and abrasive tips for grinding and polishing. In wood design, the tool can be used for engraving shallow surface decoration, and for sanding hard-to-reach spots like the grooves in a design of chip carving. Like the jigsaw, the motor-tool is effective only on small designs and soft wood. Most of the machines sold through hardware dealers are designed for hobby use and are grossly underpowered; they will not be permanently effective for use in wood design. If you can buy a motor-tool that turns at least 25,000 revolutions per minute, and can be fixed into a stationary framework, or jig, then it will be effective. The framework holds the tool rigid so that the design can be moved under the tool. This way the tool will not slip and slide

across the wood. A sliding cutting bit, out of control, can cause irreparable damage to a design. For this reason, any purchase of a motor-tool should include a high-powered machine and a stationary framework to go along with it. With both of these things under control, it's possible to "carve" by machine intricately embellished surface decoration that resembles chip carving in appearance.

As another word of caution, there are jigsaws on the market equipped with flexible power take-off shafts that hold the same bits as the motor-tool. These units operate off the side of an already underpowered jigsaw. My advice is to stay clear of buying one of these units. I have no doubt that they are delightful for building birdhouses, but they have no practical use in cutting and shaping wood. It's a child's toy for doing a man-sized job.

Other electrical tools

A number of other electrical tools are available to save labor, especially when working on larger designs. The prime consideration in purchasing any electrical tool is to buy quality, and to buy machines for heavy duty work.

A sabre saw on small designs can do the work of a jigsaw, but with the added flexibility of being portable. A portable power hacksaw, such as a *Sawzall* by *Milwaukee*, is an excellent tool for sawing thick lumber on large designs. The power hacksaw is held like a tommy-gun, requiring two hands, but it can easily slice through a two-inch plank. The pieces by Anne Arnold on page 107, and by Jane Teller on the frontis page were both cut in outline with a power hacksaw.

If your pocketbook is deep enough, electric and belt sanding machines can reduce finishing labor, while at the same time opening doors to new possibilities in design. For example, an electric portable grinding wheel, equipped with a coarse wood abrasive, can literally shape wood by brute force. The flowing sensation in the laminated piece by sculptor George Sugarman on page 109 was helped along by using a power sander in the shaping.

Holding tools

Holding tools are used to hold the design rigid while it's being worked on. The vice, which was discussed in Chapter 1, the C clamp, the bench screw, the hand screw, and the pipe or bar clamp are all holding tools.

The C clamp

The C clamp—illustrated in Figure 35—is sold by the length and width of the throat opening. The C clamp can be either fastened directly to the design, as in Figure 36, or if the design is too large, it can be fastened to a board which is screwed with wood screws to the base of the design. The clamp then holds the design rigid by holding the base board firm to the bench. If the C clamp is applied directly to the design, it should be cushioned, as illustrated in Figure 36, or it will leave a mark on the wood. Several C clamps may be necessary to hold larger pieces rigid.

The bench screw

The bench screw holds a design rigid by coming up through the bench work surface and attaching itself by threads into the base of the design. Figure 35 illustrates a bench screw, and Figure 36 illustrates the bench screw set properly in use. If a bench screw is not available, a very heavy lag screw, purchased from any hardware store, will accomplish the same result if used with a large washer.

The hand screw

The hand screw, illustrated in Figure 39, is a holding device with wooden jaws that produce an even distribution of pressure on either flat or angular work. One jaw of the hand screw may be positioned to overlap the other, where conditions on the design make this desirable. The hand screw can be used alone or it can be easily clamped to the bench.

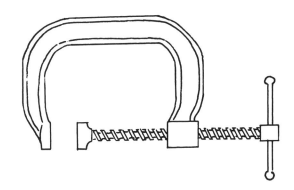

Figure 35 *The* C *clamp.*

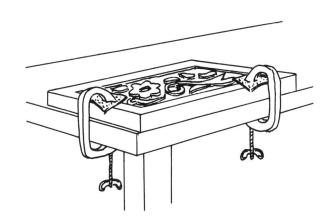

Figure 36 *Two* C *clamps in position, holding a design to the work surface of the bench. Note the use of the buffer material between the clamp and the wood.*

Figure 37 *A bench screw.*

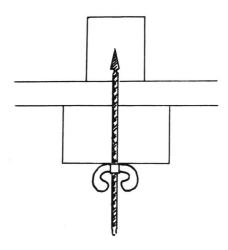

Figure 38 *A bench screw positioned on a work-bench, the arrow tip of the screw, as shown in this cross section, is imbedded in the base of the design.*

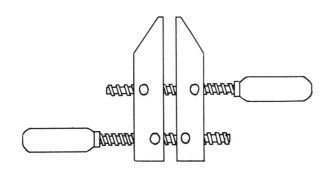

Figure 39 *A hand screw which produces an even distribution of pressure in holding.*

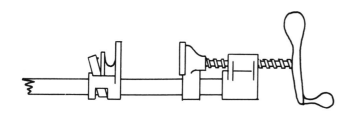

Figure 40 *A pipe, or bar clamp, for use on inter-changeable threaded lengths of pipe.*

The pipe or bar clamp

The pipe, also called the bar clamp, is illustrated in Figure 40. It consists of a set of fixtures that can be mounted to a threaded pipe of any length. A variety of pipe lengths will give you a variety of clamps using the same fixtures. If you plan to work on thick pieces, or glued laminated designs that are too long to fit between the jaws of an ordinary C clamp, a set of pipe or bar clamps is an absolute necessity. With a variety of pipe lengths, it gives you a set of selective jaw openings.

Protective devices

In wrapping up this chapter on tools, in scratching around to see if there is anything I've missed, this last point may sound elementary, but it's essential. The cuts and calluses you get on your hands are both built-in occupational hazards of wood design. The discomfort from these two ills is not something to sneer at, especially if you do any prolonged work where there is continued irritation of an already existing sore. One school of thought is to suffer the discomfort and toughen up your hands, but there are some helpers available. If you're carving with a knife and moving the blade toward you with your thumb for a stop, it will help to put a heavy Band-Aid around the end of your thumb with the pad facing your palm. This simple Band-Aid will save your thumb from a good many nicks, although it might prove a bit bulky to wear while working. Take your pick, it's either the nicks or the Band-Aid.

The palm of the hand may also become irritated when you use it as the source of pressure on the handle of a cutting tool. I've found that a golfer's glove, the type without fingers, provides excellent protection for the palm.

If you do any serious chip carving, the first knuckle of your index finger will develop a whopping callus. I've tried a Band-Aid over this knuckle, but it makes you feel like you're wearing overshoes at a ballet. Enduring the discomfort is the only solution I have to offer for that one.

Cradle by G. E. Redfield. 34″ high x 35″ long x 23″ wide; Walnut. The curved portions are cut on the curve, not bent. The piece has an oil finish. Photo courtesy of The American Craftsman's Council.

3 / Wood

Every piece of wood has special characteristics of its own which make it unique. Characteristics in wood are a kind of personality; or better yet, a set of fingerprints: no two species and no two pieces of wood within a species (or even within the same tree) are identical.

What are the characteristics of wood?

Here are some of the characteristics of wood: color; degree of hardness or softness when worked with hand tools; decay resistance; shrinkage; grain figure; elasticity in bending; texture; stringiness; odor; durability. Still other characteristics include weight, moisture content, and the way in which a given piece of wood will react to stain, fillers, and transparent finishes.

You learn to identify wood characteristics through experience; trial and error. One good way to begin identification is to drop around to your local lumber dealer and gather up scraps from a variety of wood species. Experiment with them, and compare similarities. But, most of all, compare differences.

The table in this chapter lists twenty-two types of wood readily found throughout the United States. The table lists a number of wood characteristics related to the problems of design. There are hundreds of species found in the United States. There are also dozens of sub-species within several general species; for example, Sugar Pine, Eastern Pine, Jack Pine, Lodgepole Pine, Ponderosa Pine, and Red Pine are all members of the Pine family. The list, then, is limited to the more common species. If you need a complete breakdown on all species found in the United States write: Superintendent of Documents, G.P.O., Washington, D.C., 20250, and ask for Agriculture Handbook No. 72, entitled, *Wood Handbook, Basic Information On Wood As A Material Of Construction With Data For Its Use In Design And Specification.* A minimum charge is made for this book. The table also footnotes six species of imported and exotic wood widely used in wood design.

Mobile by the author. 16″ diameter, pierced carving; Masonite fibreboard, painted black enamel. Pieces cut out on a band saw and chamfered on the edges with a wood rasp. Photo by Dave Congalton.

Wood is commercially classified as either hardwood or softwood. With admitted exception, this commercial breakdown compares the density and weight in a given species of wood against the density and weight in other species. Hardwood is generally heavier, harder, denser, less porous, less likely to shrink, more durable, and more elastic than softwood. Softwood, on the other hand, is generally the antithesis of hardwood.

Plywood and Masonite

In addition to natural wood, plywood and Masonite are both widely used by contemporary wood designers in making structural and geometric constructions. Plywood consists of sheets of thin wood laminated together in layers with glue. It runs anywhere from two layers up to several layers in thickness. Masonite, on the other hand, is a fiberboard made of steam-exploded wood fiber. Both plywood and Masonite are flexible and can be bent; one sculptor I know uses a thin Italian plywood that is so flexible he is able to bend it under the hot water faucet in his bathroom shower. Several pieces illustrated in this book were constructed with plywood as a sub-structure. The mobile illustrated on page 73 was constructed from Masonite.

How to use wood characteristics

A well executed design will capitalize on the ingrown, or built-in characteristics of wood. When planning your design, it's important to think in terms of how you can best subsidize the end result by allowing the design to use the wood and, on the other hand, the wood to enhance the design. There is a definitive give and take; the wood can suggest changes in design, changes that will make the design a stronger statement, and the design, on the other hand, may be so strong in itself that it will suggest the type of wood to be used.

As an example, Oak is a very hard and tough wood; it radiates this toughness visually. If the mood of a given design is to convey the feeling of strength, then Oak would work hard to enhance the design and the mood of strength. A piece of pulpy Balsam Fir, used on the same design, would kill any suggestion of strength because Balsam not only looks and feels flimsy, but *is* flimsy.

Another example would be in making use of natural color to carry out the theme of the design statement. The abstract wall assemblage on page 58 is entitled *Integration*. To carry out the theme of harmony in the blending of races, natural wood color was used to act out its own part in the design; a combination of White Basswood, Yellow Birch, Black Walnut, and Red Cedar was used and mounted on an aged weathered plank.

A third example in this mutual give and take of coordinating wood and design is the characteristics of grain, or grain figure. A pattern of prominent flowing grain fibers, evenly spaced like waves on water, can be made to work within design to strengthen a statement of rhythm. Straight grain, on the other hand, might suggest a feeling of calm. Erratic grain might suggest anything from subtle whimsy, to that of danger, confusion, suspense, or even terror.

And still another example of how to incorporate specific wood character into design is the use of natural decay resistance. The presence of decay resistance might be adapted for use within design against the natural elements, for preserving wood in contact with food, and for designs subject to extensive handling. For example, a piece of outdoor sculpture in Redwood will outlast the same piece executed in Pine because the wood itself works to preserve the design; Redwood is more decay resistant than Pine.

These have been only four examples. There are countless others. If you make wood work, it will help you say whatever it is you're trying to say. In this way, a designer gains double use from his medium; he works with his medium and his medium provides a bonus, a bonus of personality. Bear this in mind when you consider wood.

Culculine by Christopher Wilmarth, 1966. 32″ x 84″; made from Fir plywood, tempered Swedish Masonite, and finished with Nitrocellulous lacquers. Photo courtesy of the artist.

Expansion and contraction in wood

Wood breathes. It has pores like human skin. A once-living tree, now sawed into boards or crafted into sculpture, continues to breathe. This breathing is a constant exchange of moisture from the atmosphere: either absorbing (inhaling), or evaporating (exhaling). When wood absorbs moisture, it expands; when it dries, the wood contracts. This process—the inhaling and exhaling of moisture—never stops, even after a piece of sculpture has been completed, sealed with finish, and stands as a work of art in a gallery.

One example of what happens in this exchange of moisture—or this breathing of wood—is found in every household which uses forced air heat. In winter, cupboard doors shrink, bang shut, actually seem a size too small for the opening. In summer, especially during the rainy season, these same doors stick, have to be forced shut even though they may be heavily sealed with paint or varnish. The wood substance in these doors is breathing, it is exchanging moisture with the atmosphere; the presence or absence of moisture caused the expansion or contraction. Because wood does breathe, it must be carefully seasoned before putting it to use in design.

Seasoning

Seasoning is a process of aging wood; drying it to a point where it will remain relatively constant in moisture content. Moisture is actually the presence of sap in the wood. Drying reduces weight; decreases the risk of checking, warping, and shrinkage; reduces the likelihood of fungus attack on the wood; improves the wood's ability to hold paint, and to absorb preservatives.

Integration by the author. Relief; 14″ x 30″; White Pine, Yellow Birch, Red Cedar, and Black Walnut mounted on a weathered board, natural finish. Photo by Dave Congalton.

Seasoning is accomplished either through a natural air drying, or by an unnatural forced process of oven, or kiln drying. Wood dried in a kiln is dried by controlled heat, either electric or steam. The wood is stacked in the kiln so that air is able to freely circulate around exposed surfaces, especially around grain ends. Commercial wood sold through dealerships is almost always kiln dried and is ready for immediate use in design. Don't try drying wood at home in the oven; it's too dangerous.

If you prefer the natural process of air drying, or of selecting wood from standing trees, then your motto should read: "plan ahead, and stockpile." Air drying takes months, sometimes a year or longer. If you don't plan ahead and stockpile, you'll never have the wood available when you want it, and if you're like I am, when you want it, you want it loudly.

Air drying should be done at an even pace, preferably outside under a covered shed to avoid shocking the wood. Too much sun too quickly may cause the wood to split. Splitting, whether in great wide cavities or shallow surface checks, can cause unnecessary waste of valuable wood. On the other hand, if the presence of splits and checks challenges your eye, you may want to incorporate them into your design. The piece illustrated on page 57 uses natural splits to the advantage of the design.

Air dried wood should be piled so that air can freely circulate around the exposed outer surfaces. Air drying can be hastened on large pieces by boring a hole up into the wood from the base. This hole tends to equalize the exterior seasoning by letting some moisture escape from inside; the hole acts like an air chimney. In order to tell when air dried lumber is ready for use, you pretty much have to judge for yourself according to the way it feels, its weight, its appearance, and how a cutting tool moves through it. Technically speaking, for the United States as a whole, the average moisture content of thoroughly air dried lumber runs around 15–18 percent. You'll have no way

of accurately measuring the moisture content except to feel the wood, weigh its heft in your hand, make certain that no sap is visible, and test the wood with your tool. Once you make a slice into it, if there's no sap and if the wood is light in color, the wood is probably dry enough to use.

Problem characteristics

There are a number of natural and induced characteristics of wood that, depending upon your point of view, can prove to be either a problem or a challenge. Before you run away from these characteristics, at least look them over to see if they might not be incorporated in your design.

Stringy wood fiber. Stringiness of fiber is one characteristic to look out for. It is sometimes found in Fir, Butternut, Elm, and occasionally in Oak. When wood is stringy, the fibers respond as if they were an accumulation of separate threads, each thread remaining independent of the whole. This characteristic of stringiness is much like opening an electric cable and finding, instead of a uniform interior texture, a nest of separate smaller wires each with its own insulated coating.

The blade of a cutting tool running *across* the fibers in a stringy piece of wood responds much like bouncing a stick across the staves of a picket fence; the blade of the tool bobs as if cutting across mountains and valleys. In order to make an even cut *across* stringy fiber, you'll need a sharp tool, plus a bit of extra downward pressure on the high points. A cut made *with* the grain on a stringy piece of wood may be difficult to control because the fibers will want to pull out like separate guitar strings and follow their own course rather than the course you had intended. If this happens, keep the blade of the tool headed *into* the fiber rather

than between the layers of fiber; make sure you're *cutting* the fiber rather than running with it. Stringiness is usually visible. If it can be seen, you might make use of it by adapting it to a design of rhythm through the repetition in line.

Pitch and wood rot. Once in a while a chunk of wood will continually ooze pitch (a sticky yellow sap). About all you can do with pitch is to cut it out, hope it will dry, or try to seal it with something like shellac. Wood rot is another potential problem that you occasionally run into when you get beneath the exposed surface. One way to deal with wood rot is to cut it out and fill the empty hole with wood filler. Another way (and this includes dealing with pitch), is to revise your design to make use of the unexpected hole. That surface hole might prove to be just what was needed in your design.

Knots. Knots are a common characteristic of certain softwoods, especially Pine and Cedar. A knot is the base of a branch that grew out from within the wood substance. It interrupts the flow of grain by a tight swirling figure of unusually hard wood. Because a knot was the root of a separate branch, it may contract quicker in drying than the wood around it. When this happens, it might pop out, leaving a hole, even in a finished piece. Check the knots in wood to see that they are sound and solid. Often they can be glued in place or packed with wood filler. Before discarding a knotty piece of wood, see if you are receptive to the challenge of using those knots in your design.

Burls. Burls are knotty outgrowths on growing trees. If they are sound, they often contain the most exotic figuring found in the tree. For this reason, many designers covet them. Burl bowls, for example, are a prize possession among collectors. Burls are not as easy to work with as the straight growth of the tree; the wood is tougher. If the design calls for movement, the grain of a burl really flows.

Antiquing and weathering. Antiquing and weath-

Bikini by William H. Wilson. 42″ high; made from a found piece of Oak. Other than a slight padding on the breast and buttocks, sanding, and the addition of the bikini, the artist left this natural form intact. Photo courtesy of the artist.

A comparative, and selective list showing properties and design characteristics of woods grown in the United States. For a more complete list, write: Superintendent of Documents, G.P.O., Washington, D.C. 20250, and ask for Agriculture Handbook No. 72, entitled, *Wood Handbook, Basic Information On Wood As A Material Of Construction With Data For Its Use In Design And Specification.* Abbreviations used: H. is hardwood, S. is softwood, and M-L is moderate to low.

COMMON NAME	WHERE FOUND	COLOR	EASE OF WORKING WITH HAND TOOLS	RESISTANCE TO DECAY	HARD OR SOFT CLASS	VOLUME % SHRINKAGE FR. GREEN TO 20%	USE IN DESIGN	SPECIAL CHARACTERISTICS
ALDER	PACIFIC COAST	PALE PINKISH BROWN	EASY	M-L	H	4.2%	FURNITURE	LOW SHOCK RESISTANCE
WHITE ASH	GREAT LAKES MID. ATL.	GRAYISH BROWN	TOUGH, HARD	M-L	H	4.5%	FURNITURE	HEAVY, STRONG, & STIFF
ASPEN	N. EAST GREAT LAKES	LIGHT BROWN	EASY	M-L	H	3.9%	MOBILE & PRACTICE BLOCKS	LIGHT, SOFT, & LOW IN STRENGTH ODORLESS AROUND FOOD
BASSWOOD	GREAT LAKES MID. ATL. CENTRAL	CREAMY BROWN	EASY SOFT	M-L	H	5.3%	SCULPTURE CH. CARVING WHITTLING	EVEN TEXTURE, VERY LITTLE GRAIN FIGURE
BEECH	MID. ATL. CENTRAL	REDDISH WHITE	TOUGH	M-L	H	5.4%	TABLEWARE	PRODUCES SMOOTH FINISH GOOD FOR STEAM BENDING
BIRCH, YELLOW	N. EAST GREAT LAKES	YELLOW- LT. BROWN	TOUGH, HARD	M-L	H	5.6%	TABLEWARE, TURNED WOOD PRODUCTS	HEAVY SHRINKAGE, EVEN TEXTURE, GOOD FOR AROUND FOOD, SUCH AS FORKS, SPOONS, & BUTTER MOLDS
BUTTERNUT	N. EAST	COCOA BROWN	EASY	M-L	H	3.5%	SCULPTURE	GOOD GRAIN FIGURE JUST A BIT STRINGY
CEDAR, ALASKA	N. WEST	YELLOW	EASY, SOFT	HIGH	S	3.1%	SCULPTURE	STRAIGHT GRAINED UNPLEASANT ODOR
CEDAR, N. WHITE	GREAT LAKES N. EAST	PINK	EASY, SOFT	HIGH	S	2.4%	SCULPTURE	PLEASANT ODOR
NOTE: THERE ARE MANY OTHER VARIETIES OF CEDAR SUITABLE FOR SCULPTURE, SIMILAR IN CHARACTERISTICS TO THE ABOVE TWO								
CHERRY, BLACK	EASTERN U.S.	REDDISH BROWN	TOUGH, HARD	M-L	H	3.8%	SCULPTURE	GOOD GRAIN FIGURE SMOOTHES WELL
ELM, AMERICAN	EASTERN U.S.	LIGHT GRAY, RED TINGE	TOUGH, HARD	M-L	H	4.9%	LARGE SCULPTURE	GOOD GRAIN FIGURE, EXCELLENT FOR BENDING, DOESN'T SPLINTER
ELM, SLIPPERY	EASTERN U.S.	DK. BROWN, RED TINGE	TOUGH, HARD	M-L	H	4.6%	SCULPTURE	SOFTER THAN AMERICAN ELM GOOD GRAIN FIGURE
NOTE: THERE ARE MANY OTHER VARIETIES OF ELM SUITABLE FOR SCULPTURE, SIMILAR IN CHARACTERISTICS TO THE ABOVE TWO								

Wood	Source	Color	Workability	Size	S/H	%	Uses	Characteristics
FIR, BALSAM	EASTERN U.S.	CREAMY WHITE	EASY	M-L	S	3.7%	MOBILES & PRACTICE	VERY SOFT TEXTURE REQUIRES SHARP TOOLS OR IT CRUSHES
NOTE: THERE ARE MANY OTHER VARIETIES OF FIR SUITABLE FOR CARVING, SIMILAR IN CHARACTERISTICS TO THE ABOVE								
HACKBERRY	SOUTH & S. ATLANTIC	YELLOW-GREEN-GRAY	TOUGH	M-L	H	5.6%	FURNITURE	RESEMBLES ELM IN STRUCTURE
HOLLY, AMERICAN	ATLANTIC, GULF COAST	WHITE	MEDIUM TO EASY	M-L	H	5.6%	MUSICAL INST. SCULPTURE INLAY	CUTS SMOOTHLY FOR FINE DETAIL, AND IS GOOD FOR DYES AND STAINS
MAPLE, SUGAR	EASTERN U.S.	COCOA BROWN	TOUGH, HARD	M-L	H	5.0%	SCULPTURE FURNITURE CH. CARVING	FINE, UNIFORM TEXTURE, AND STRAIGHT GRAIN
NOTE: THERE ARE MANY OTHER VARIETIES OF MAPLE SUITABLE FOR SCULPTURE, SIMILAR IN CHARACTERISTICS TO THE ABOVE								
OAK, WHITE	EASTERN U.S.	GRAYISH BROWN, WITH RED TINGE	TOUGH, HARD	M-L	H	5.3%	LARGE SCULPTURE, FURNITURE	GOOD GRAIN FIGURE. NEEDS BOLD TREATMENT, AND SHARP TOOLS
NOTE: THERE ARE MANY OTHER VARIETIES OF OAK SUITABLE FOR SCULPTURE, SIMILAR IN CHARACTERISTICS TO THE ABOVE								
PINE, EASTERN WHITE	EASTERN U.S.	CREAM TO LIGHT BROWN	EASY	M-L	S	2.7%	SCULPTURE LAMINATION CH. CARVING	UNIFORM TEXTURE STRAIGHT GRAIN IDEAL FOR GLUING
PINE, SUGAR	WEST COAST	BUFF	EASY	M-L	S	2.6%	SCULPTURE LAMINATION CH. CARVING	UNIFORM TEXTURE, STRAIGHT GRAIN, LOW SHRINKAGE, LARGE PIECES
NOTE: THERE ARE MANY OTHER VARIETIES OF PINE SUITABLE FOR SCULPTURE, SIMILAR IN CHARACTERISTICS TO THE ABOVE TWO								
SYCAMORE, AMERICAN	CENTRAL & EAST STATES	FLESH BROWN	MEDIUM TO EASY	M-L	H	4.7%	SCULPTURE FURNITURE VENEER	FINE TEXTURE INTERLOCKED GRAIN
REDWOOD	CALIFORNIA	CHERRY TO BROWNISH RED	MEDIUM TO EASY	HIGH	S	2.4%	OUTDOOR SCULPTURE, FURNITURE	AVAILABLE IN LARGE PIECES, STRAIGHT GRAINED. RESISTS DECAY
WALNUT, BLACK	CENTRAL & EAST STATES	COCOA BROWN	MEDIUM TO EASY	HIGH	H	4.3%	SCULPTURE FURNITURE	STRAIGHT GRAIN, WELL SUITED TO NATURAL FINISH, EASILY WORKED

Note: A number of imported woods available from wood supply dealers are equally well suited to sculpture, chip carving, lamination, and other design techniques. *Ebony*, found in Gabon, Africa, is inky black in color, close grained, very hard, and polishes brilliantly. *Mahogany*, a cinnamon colored softer wood grown in India and Africa, is relatively easy to work with hand tools. *Brazilian Tulipwood, Indian Teak,* and *European Pearwood* are also excellent for fine detail in sculpture. *African Zebra Wood* is an exotic, richly figured wood with a fire-flame grain ideal for work where grain pattern can make its own dominant statement.

ering are a combination of applied and induced characteristics in wood which can add greatly to design. Old weathered wood, when used in a manner that preserves its appearance, can complement the right design, can in fact give a design a feeling of authenticity. Antiquing can also be induced through texture strokes, through forced weathering, and—as in certain colonial furnitures—through reproduced wormholes and sand-blasted surfaces. My own prejudices don't agree with the processes of reproduced wormholes and sand-blasted surfaces, but I must admit to having seen pieces where this induced effect was carried off very well.

Bill Wilson's *Bikini*, illustrated on page 60 was made from a found, natural Elm branch. Bill found this branch in the pasture below his studio. The branch dictated its own design to Bill's eye. He added one breast and a bit of padding on the buttocks. Otherwise (exclusive of bikini), the piece is just as he found it. The natural cracks in the wood complement the lengthy, twiggy rhythm in the torso.

How to select your wood

I would suggest you begin with softwood and work up to hard as your skill increases. There's absolutely no point in beginning on a chunk of Ebony when Pine will generate the confidence that Ebony would steal. It's my suggestion also that you plan your designs, using wood indigenous to the area in which you live. If you live in Iowa and must depend upon wood from Gaboon, Africa, then you're in for some expensive nervous indigestion, not to mention waiting. Why not stick with wood that is fairly common to your own area? If you do want to experiment with exotic woods, the suppliers listed at the back of the book will be able to send you information on species, costs, and sizes.

George Washington on horseback, circa 1785. Carved and painted on polychrome, 21″ long x 24½″ high. Photo by Einars J. Mengis; courtesy Shelburne Museum.

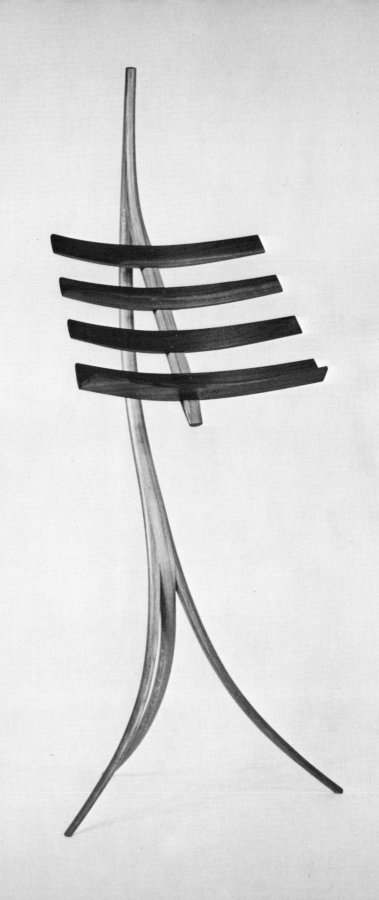

4 / Design

"Since Rodin's time there has arisen what is virtually a new art, a concept of a piece of sculpture as a three dimensional mass occupying space and only to be apprehended by senses that are <u>alive</u> to its volume and ponderability, as well as to its visual appearance."

Sir Herbert Read, *The Art of Sculpture*

The key word in the above quotation, as underscored, is the word *alive*. The wood designer must develop an electric, sensual perception if he is to create original design; his eyes, fingertips, ears, nose, and tongue must be *alive* to the physical world around him. His senses must be free to absorb and to safely tuck away shapes, textures, smells, sounds, and tastes as stimulants for future reference. Wendell Castle's music stand, illustrated on the facing page, proves that the artist interpreted this piece of functional sculpture with the acute use of all of his senses. The piece literally sings, and moves with rhythm. It is *alive*; so were the senses of its designer.

You will remember from the introduction, that the Greek word for design means poetry. In a sense, the wood designer must, then, interpret the world as if he were a three dimensional poet. It is not his task to reproduce the world, but to *interpret* the world; he uses his vision to dig: to dig out what lies below and ahead of the surface.

Painting is a two dimensional medium of height and width, where the third dimension of depth is implied by creating a visual *illusion* on a flat surface. The wood designer, on the other hand, is concerned with mass or depth as a physical *reality*. The block of wood, the stick, the construction of parts is no illusion. Depth or mass must be dealt with in full.

The principles of design

The principles of design, for the purposes of this text, include *balance, rhythm, emphasis, unity,* and *function*. These principles are the "laws" of

Music stand by Wendell Castle. 55″ high; laminated Oak and Rosewood; designed for the 13th Triennale in Milan, Italy. Rhythm here is the obvious statement. Mr. Castle tries to produce a synthesis or metamorphosis of natural forms. They are not free form, but are constructed within the strict boundaries of the scale, the material, and the necessary function the object must perform. Photo courtesy of the artist.

design; the internal structure by which design is visually represented. Each of these principles will be dealt with separately in this chapter. Because they appear in a separate paragraph on the page does not mean to suggest that they are independent of each other. On the contrary, there is an involved, continuous interaction between all of these principles; a blending together as they work within any given design.

The ingredients that build principles

In addition to the principles of design, there are still other components of design. I call these additional components the *ingredients* of design. They include *color, line, tone, composition, form,* and *texture.* They are the raw materials, the ingredients which work to build the principles.

Rhythm, as one of the principles of design, for example, can be rendered through any one or combination of ingredients. As ingredients, wood *color,* design *lines,* surface *tone* shading, the *composition* of parts, the placement of *forms,* and surface *texture* can each build rhythm, or can be combined together to build rhythm. A flowing series of grain *lines* on a piece of Pine used in sculpture can suggest rhythm. In the same manner, a surface *texture* can be carved to create the sensation of rhythm. Or even the *composition* of several pieces of wood as positioned within a whole piece can suggest rhythm.

Balance, like rhythm, can also be stated through the ingredients of color, line, tone, composition, form, and texture. And this is equally true of emphasis as a principle. Ingredients of design, then, are the building materials; principles of design are what you do with those ingredients.

Making selections

Making selections is an essential part of design. Behind a delicious recipe there is an excellent chef. Behind a successful design there is a sensitive designer. A chef exercises selection over his ingre-

dients in order to build his recipe. He must choose specific ingredients with which to bake a given cake. Cakes all contain ingredients in common, such as flour, but a raisin cake does not contain the same ingredients as a chocolate cake. The chef selects those ingredients necessary to bake a raisin cake; he selects raisins as an ingredient over chocolate.

A designer, in the same manner, must exercise selection over the ingredients that make up his design. Two sculptures in wood might both build a statement around rhythm as a principle of design, but one might emphasize the ingredients of line and texture while the other emphasizes the ingredients of composition and color; the designer has made a selection of his *dominant* ingredients, although many of these ingredients are present in some sense.

In order to make a selection, a chef must *know* the ingredients available to him, and what they will produce when combined in a recipe for the cake. In order to make a selection, a wood designer must *know* the ingredients of wood design available to him and what they will represent when combined in a piece of sculpture. If a chef uses a pinch of everything, he'll come up with nothing but unpalatable garbage; he must select and eliminate from practical knowledge. Garlic powder doesn't belong in a raisin cake and the chef knows this.

If a wood designer tries to build a strong statement by throwing in a little of everything, he'll come up with visual chaos. A round red dot painted on a wooden cube doesn't suggest rhythm; the designer knows this because he is intimately familiar with what rhythm is, and how to combine ingredients to build rhythm. Familiarity and knowledge are essential for selection. The designer may elect not to use all the ingredients in a given design; he may emphasize only one, several independently, or combine many. The end result, the whole design, is a process of selection and elimination based upon knowledge.

Selection is more often unconscious and intui-

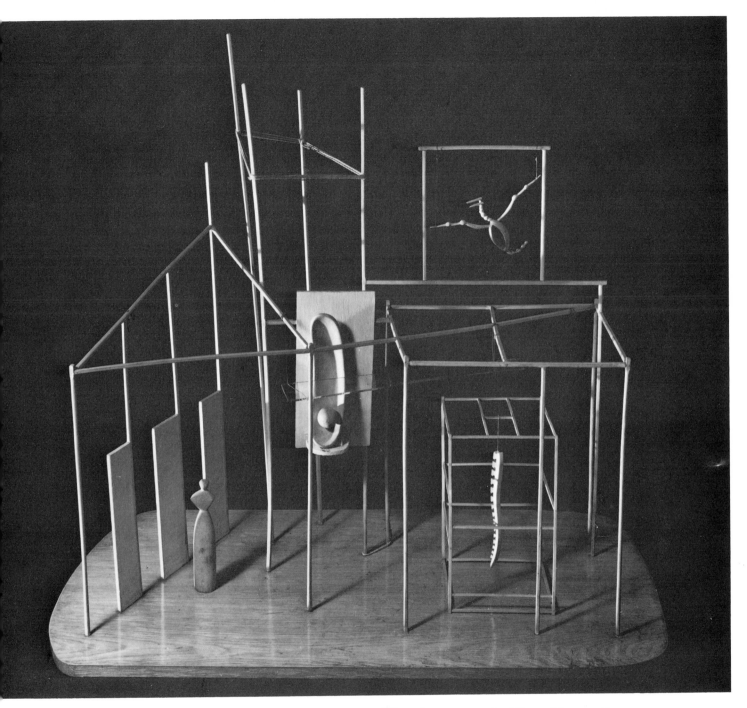

The palace at 4 a.m. by Alberto Giacometti, 1932-33. 25″ high, 28¼″ wide, 15¾″ deep; construction in wood, glass, wire, and string. The sculptor here fixes the placement of objects on a platform and builds a frame-like environment around the figures, in an attempt to exercise some control over space. Photo by Herbert Matter; collection, The Museum of Modern Art, New York.

Two forms by Henry Moore, 1934. 11″ high; Pynkado wood. Asymmetrical balance gained through the hollow, roof-like larger form. The hole in the larger form gives visual reality to three dimensional design. Collection, The Museum of Modern Art, New York, gift of Sir Michael Sadler.

tive than it is conscious and procedural. The designer does not sit down and ponder a long list of design principles and ingredients in order to make his selection. He makes his selection spontaneously because he knows what it takes to build the design in his mind. A critic or admirer might come along, look at a given design and say: "Ah, this piece has a strong feeling of rhythm, and it was built by a subtle combination of grain lines and surface texture." This critic or admirer is labeling and defining the piece for his own reference; he is consciously dissecting what he sees. The sculptor, on the other hand, may not have consciously defined and labeled the ingredients of his piece because the process of designing *is* spontaneous; the designer selects intuitively. Because he does not ponder the list of labeled principles and ingredients, is not to suggest that he doesn't know where he's headed. On the contrary, he knows exactly where he's going, even if he's experimenting, because principles and ingredients are his business.

Space and placement

Before discussing each of the principles of design separately, and how design ingredients build principles, it's essential to view the design externally in terms of space and placement.

What exactly is it that creates the total impact of a three dimensional form? First, there is the form itself, the mass, be it a piece of sculpture, a wall relief, or an article of furniture.

Second, there is the space immediately around (and sometimes within) the form—space which sets off and silhouettes the form and convinces the eye that the form has mass. The space immediately around the silhouette of the form is referred to as *negative* space. This negative space is an integral part of the form; in a sense it is attached to the form because every form carries its negative space with it (like a hole in a doughnut) wherever it goes.

Third, there is the *placement* of that form in

its environment—a wall, a room, a field—a specific space in which the form is seen by the viewer. For example, when a relief is mounted against an uncluttered 10′ x 12′ white wall, or a piece of sculpture stands in a corner of a room, the wall or room becomes an environmental space. The form, the space immediately around the form, and the eventual placement of the form in a specific environmental space as seen by the viewer—all combine to create the total impact of a three dimensional piece.

Think now of an orange sitting on a table six feet away from you. First there is the rounded orange; then there is the rounded space immediately around the edge of that orange; and then there is the total space of the table and the room in which you are looking at that orange. It takes all three to make that orange real. The orange does not exist alone. The orange must interact with space—both negative and environmental—before it can be a three dimensional orange.

This discussion is not meant as a merry-go-round of "which came first, the chicken or the egg." On the contrary, it's an attempt to pull your thinking away from the object itself and consider the object in terms of space and placement in a setting.

Space and placement are inseparable in design; one cannot exist without the other. There is a mutual dependence and involvement between space and placement. The wood designer can make an impact on space, and he can also exercise areas of control over the placement of his designs as they are seen by others.

Since negative space (the space immediately around and within the form) travel with the form wherever it goes, the designer permanently controls negative space by the lines of his design. The way in which he controls negative space is what makes his design unique. He may tiptoe into negative space gently by rhythmic flowing lines, or he may prefer boldly crashing into negative space by ripping it into parts with erratic lines.

A hole, or series of openings within a form, divides negative space into permanent parts and

therefore controls it, and also adds credibility to the visual existence of mass. The hole, or series of openings, makes the viewer aware of mass because it lets in light, shadow, and tone. The mobile on page 54 uses an outer circle to set limits to the negative space immediately around the design. The inner pieces cut the remainder of negative space into parts. And the figures on page 100 also control negative space within the form by pierced openings between the figures. How else can the designer affect space and placement?

The size of an object is one way to affect space and placement. Sculptor Henry Moore has always been concerned with size. One of his large pieces is likely to begin by being very small, perhaps even small enough to hold in the hand. He feels an intimacy with his figure when it is small; he is close to it, can grasp it visually and emotionally without great effort. Even his larger designs very likely began as small intimate hand forms.

A large design, on the other hand, has its own way of demanding attention—such as the seven story stabile by Alexander Calder at the World's Fair in Montreal. You can't miss that piece. It's so large that it has a way of grabbing you in off the street, shouting: "Here I am, come and look at me!" Mr. Calder's stabile would not fit in your living room, and Mr. Moore's hand form would have no place outdoors in a World's Fair. Size, then, can affect both space and placement.

A controlled environment around a wood design can also affect space and placement. Alberto Giacometti very often constructed an environment around his sculpture in order to exercise some control over the distance between his piece and the viewer. In *The Palace at 4:00 a.m.* (page 69), he constructed a frame around his figures. The frame establishes a perspective relationship be-

Tryst #2 by Doris Chase. 102" high; laminated wood. This sculptor designs and finishes her own pieces, but has the lamination done for her. This is a movable form; a rectangular solid that comes apart and involves the viewer in space and placement. Photo courtesy of the artist.

tween the figures and the outer limits of the frame; it controls a specific piece of space by creating a frame environment against which the figures are viewed. Louise Nevelson (see *Night Zag IV*, page 116), on the other hand, literally creates a total environment into which the viewer is swallowed. Her large constructions very often encircle the viewer. The viewer almost walks right inside the sculpture. In these pieces, Mrs. Nevelson literally controls the physical relationship of the viewer to the sculpture.

Grouping is still another way to affect space and placement. A grouping of wooden figures or forms fixed to a platform controls the placement of those figures as they relate to each other. Henry Moore's *Two Forms* on page 70, is an example of fixed grouping. Doris Chase (see *Tryst #2* on page 72), develops another approach to space and placement through grouping. The viewer can assemble and disassemble the forms at will. She enlists the involvement of the viewer in space and placement by silently inviting him to arrange her forms to his own taste. She is concerned with space and placement, but doesn't attempt to control it. She places control in the hands of the viewer.

Space and placement are therefore important considerations in wood design. Think of your design in terms of how others will see it; what can you do, as designer, toward controlling the negative space and placement of your own piece? The old adage of not seeing the trees because of the forest has relevance here. If you get so caught up in chipping away wood, and in the physical bulk of reducing your design that you fail to see it as others see it, you may reduce the effect of your impact. Keep space and placement in mind. Use them deliberately to your advantage whenever you can.

Mobile by the author. 16″ diameter, pierced carving; Masonite fibreboard, painted black enamel. Pieces cut out on a band saw and chamfered on the edges with a wood rasp. Photo by Dave Congalton.

Balance

Balance in wood design can be stated *symmetrically, asymmetrically,* or *radially.* A simple illustration of symmetrical and asymmetrical balance is the teeter-totter or see-saw. When children of equal weight and size are placed at opposite ends, with the axis point in direct center, they produce *symmetrical* balance. If, on the other hand, a larger child is placed on one end, the axis point must be moved to one side of center if the two children are to balance each other. The balance remains intact, but we now have *asymmetrical* balance. The human body is another common example of symmetrical balance; parts and extremities are equal on either side of the torso. A man with only one leg can be asymmetrically balanced by a crutch and a slight droop of the shoulder on the side with the missing leg.

A simple illustration of *radial* balance is a child's drawing of the sun with radiating lines projecting out from a red ball representing the sun's rays. These radiating lines balance the drawing because they anchor the sun visually to the page.

Generally, symmetrical and radial balance are visually obvious. There is an equal distribution of parts or lines which one immediately recognizes. Asymmetrical balance, on the other hand, is more subtle; it is there but is not stated so emphatically, and it leaves room in designing for more freedom of exploration.

Balance in wood design, whether symmetrical or asymmetrical, can be *deliberately* developed through the placement of mass or shapes, through the presence of prominent grain, and through the application of color. Or symmetrical and asymmetrical balance can be *subtly* developed by combining one or more of these methods.

Let's look at a simple example. Two wooden

Ceremonial board (Gope), New Guinea: Papuan Gulf, Wapo Creek. 50¾″ high; painted wood. This low relief carved with child-like simplicity is an example of symmetrical balance. Photo courtesy The Museum of Primitive Art.

balls of equal size mounted at either end of a flat board create *deliberate* symmetrical balance. If one ball is exchanged for a larger ball and placed closer to the first ball, the balance remains intact and the piece is then asymmetrically balanced because the space between the larger ball and the end of the board balances the visual whole. Now if the discarded smaller ball is replaced right next to the ball of equal size, the form is visually unbalanced because there are two objects on the one side and one object on the other. But paint that large ball bright red and you once again establish an asymmetrical balance by giving the large ball the added implied weight of color. Or, if the two smaller balls had only a dull grain but the larger ball was carved from something like an exotic Zebra wood, the prominence of the grain on the larger ball would imply asymmetrical balance, even though there were two balls as against one ball in placement.

The mobile on page 73 is an example of symmetrical balance through the equal distribution of shapes. The rail openings in the old weathered fence post are equal, as are the size and mass of the three wooden ballet figures within. Other examples of symmetrical balance through equal distribution of shapes are the Gope ceremonial board on the facing page, and the marzipan mold on page 30. The Gope ceremonial board, with its child-like figure, has an equal distribution of shapes on either side of center. The marzipan mold gains symmetrical balance by the identical repetition of the eagle motif on each side of the center circle. The female standing figure, on the other hand, illustrated to the right, gains symmetrical balance both through the equal distribution of parts and the accented equal distribution of grain figure.

Standing figure, British Columbia: Kwakiutl. 50″ high; free standing wood sculpture. Vivid grain figure in this piece creates its own surface texture in rhythmic flesh. Photo courtesy The Museum of Primitive Art.

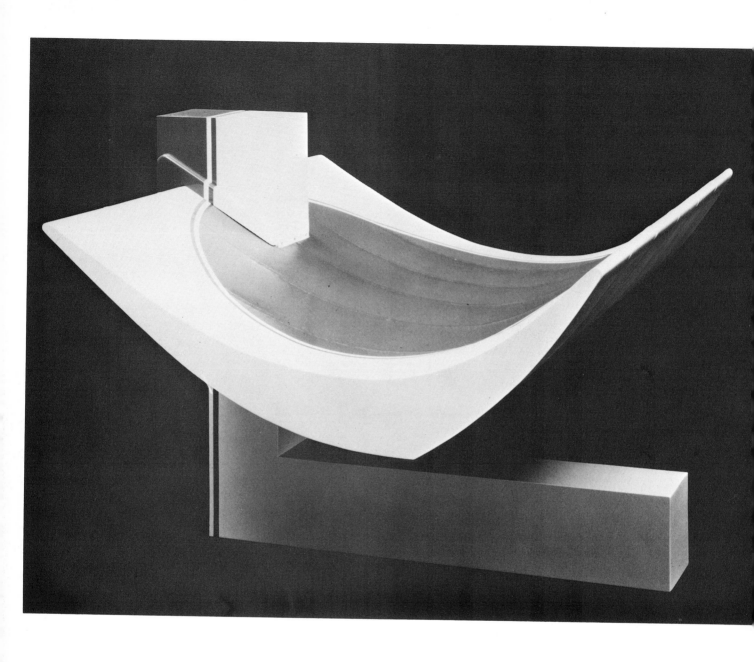

Big zero by Richard Randell, 1965. (above)
40″ x 60″ x 52″; a mixed media construction of
fabric, plywood, and enamel. The top, curved surface is
fabric covered with enamel: the rest of the piece is
painted plywood. Flight here is the theme; emphasis is
gained by the red circle against a white background.
Photo courtesy Royal S. Marks Gallery.

The globe by Mario Ceroli, 1966. (right) 5′ high
x 6′ wide. A laminated construction made from old
shipping crates. Laminated with glue and mortised.
An example of radial balance. Photo courtesy
Bonino Gallery.

76

Henry Moore's *Two Forms* on page 70 is asymmetrically balanced, even though the two forms are unequal in mass. The roof-like extension of the larger form over the smaller form and the concave indentation of the larger form that leads the eye to hug the smaller form, adds the balance. *Big Zero*, on page 76, is asymmetrically balanced by a combination of mass and color. One part of the vertical plane is painted red which adds weight and balances the design.

Mario Ceroli's *The Globe*, on page 77, is an example of radial balance in wood where equal lines extend from the center of the globe. *The Eagle With Draped Flags*, on page 79, combines symmetrical and radial balance. The distribution of shapes on either side of center is equal and the radiating lines of the draped flags are also equal. Radial balance is common to chip and surface carving where surface lines develop the design.

Another sense of balance is a matter of physical weight—center of gravity balance on free standing sculpture. If mass is not properly balanced on free standing sculpture, the design will literally topple. When planning a free standing piece, remember that the center of gravity is important to balance. Many figures, for example, are mounted on a base. A base can be positioned to offset the weight of an asymmetrically balanced piece of sculpture. Weight can also be added to the base to force center of gravity balance. On the bent figure called *Rhythm* on page 88, I wanted a slight, gentle base to reflect the lines of the design. I flared the base out on either side into a taper to balance the figure. If I had wanted the base off-center, I could have added weight to the base by cutting a groove in the under side and gluing in recessed iron nuts or similar objects of weight. Many sculptors in wood mount asymmetrically balanced figures on stone or iron to create center of gravity balance by the weight of the base. A base is a constant headache in free standing sculpture. It deserves your attention. There is a challenge in designing to blend a base with the figure so that it doesn't look as if the design were merely plopped on the

Tipsy by the author. 18″ high; Basswood. Carved in the round with an X-Acto knife, stained Fruitwood, and finished smooth with three coats of satin varnish. Here the figure works, but the base doesn't. The intent was to create a base that conflicted with the figure, anchoring an otherwise impending peril. Photo by Dave Congalton.

Eagle with draped flags, nineteenth century. 23″ tall with a 42″ wingspan. The eagle head is carved in the full round, but the emblem shield and draped flags are carved in low relief. A combination of symmetrical and radial balance. Photo by Einars J. Mengis; courtesy Shelburne Museum, Inc.

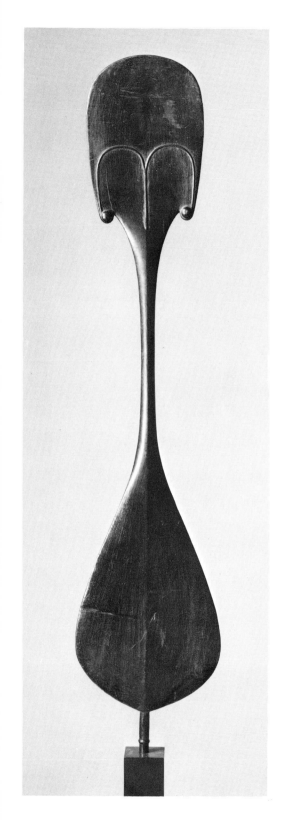

base as an afterthought.

Framing is a method of balancing an otherwise unbalanced wall relief asymmetrically. A frame sets limits to the design and can add visual weight to offset the otherwise unbalanced placements.

One cannot insist that all designs be balanced, whether symmetrically, asymmetrically, or radially, but balance is a principle to apply whenever you plan your design. If you want to break the rules to create a feeling of tension, or impending catastrophe, an unbalanced design can be very effective. But the fact remains that to *break* the rule you must first *recognize* it.

Rhythm

Rhythm in design is rendered mainly through line. Every line has energy. When you say that a Greyhound dog has swift curves, you are implying rhythm by the lines of the Greyhound's silhouette. The lines of the dog have energy and suggest rhythm.

Lines in design create an emotional impact. A horizontal line suggests calm; a diagonal line and an erratic line suggest unrest; radiating lines suggest vitality; a line that completes a circle suggests unity; a vertical line suggests dignity; a curved line suggests graceful movement. Two excellent examples of graceful movement from a gentle curved line are the Bobo seat on page 80, and the Easter Island ceremonial paddle on the same page. It would be difficult to visualize any improvement over these two outstanding examples of primitive art. Look back through some of the

---

Ceremonial paddle. Polynesia, Easter Island. (far left) 32⅞″ high; wood. This simple functional-ceremonial piece makes a strong statement of rhythm. Photo courtesy The Museum of Primitive Art.

Seat, African, Upper Volta: Bobo. (left) 22⅛″ high; wood. The clean, sweeping, tapered line of this primitive bench would easily match the most contemporary design in a functional piece. Photo courtesy The Museum of Primitive Art.

other illustrations already presented and discover for yourself how many examples of line you can identify.

An unambiguous sense of rhythm in design is rendered through the repetition of line, whether curved, erratic, or vertical. A repeated line leads the eye; it can grow from small to large, or from large to small. It has rhythm because it flows. A familiar example of rhythm in a curved line progressing from large to small is the trademark on the Continental Can Company: a large C enclosing two progressively smaller C's. Rhythm here is developed through reverse growth and repetition. The arrow weathervane on page 83 develops movement by the familiar repetition and growth of the arrow feather lines. The Kifwebe mask on the same page seems almost to dance by itself because of the repetition of curved lines. And *Victory At Sea* on page 110 illustrates the use of repeated horizontal lines in lamination to create the definite calm or "victory" of the battle that is finished. When a design has no particular visual course, when lines do not lead the eye, the design is static.

In addition to the lines of your design, rhythm in wood can be implied through repetition or growth in grain figure, through the flow of surface texture, through color, through tone, and through the placement of shapes and mass. This is true whether these elements are applied externally, or are naturally inherent in wood.

A natural grain figure that expands, that grows out from a center in a given piece of wood will lead the eye. Surface texture—shallow gouge strokes, for example—can suggest rhythm if they are arranged on the wood surface to lead the eye by repetition and direction. Color can suggest rhythm, as can tone, if it builds or progresses in depth in a gradual lighting or darkening of flow. The placement of mass or shapes can suggest rhythm when they progress in a developed order by size. A whole series of wooden balls mounted on a board and progressing in size from small to large will lead the eye toward the direction of progression: toward the larger ball.

Rhythm, then, is important to planning. Sufficient to say that if you complete a wood construction where the motif is built upon radiating lines with a title *Tranquillity*, you may be in for a fight.

Emphasis

Emphasis in design is when a particular area of the design stands out, seems to speak louder or seems to attract the eye to a particular form within the design. On a bright night with a full moon, your eye is drawn toward the moon because the moon stands out among so many other stars. In this instance, by being several thousand times brighter than the stars, the moon fixes your eye; it becomes *the* point of *emphasis* in your visual horizon.

Contrast is the means by which the wood designer uses emphasis. To create contrast means to differentiate one part, or series of parts, from the whole. Hard is a contrast of soft; rough a contrast of smooth; long a contrast of short; thick a contrast of thin; light a contrast of dark, and so on.

Contrast in wood design can be rendered through strength of line, depth of color, prominence of grain figure, change of surface texture, and through concentrated detail. In *Bardana* on page 109, most of the piece has a flowing sensation of curved lines, arcs, and gentle tapers. Suddenly, at dead center, the flow is interrupted by fan-like radiating horizontal lines that stop the flow through strength of line contrast. There is a red circle on *Big Zero*, page 76, which develops contrast through color; red against white. The swirl grain of a prominent knot can be placed within a design to draw the eye by contrast in grain character. The bowl on page 84 is an example of contrast through surface texture; the outside is left with heavy gouge marks while the inside is finished smooth. And the strawberry, chip carved into the butter print on the same page, draws the eye by developing contrast through concentrated detail. Contrast then gives emphasis, and emphasis comes with planning.

Unity

When the above principles of balance, rhythm, and emphasis are combined, a design is said to have unity. Unity comes through a harmonious blending of parts. A given design need not display all of the principles to have unity. A piece can still have unity if it reaches the eye as a total impact. If, on the other hand, the eye can catch only glimpses of a statement, then unity is missing; somehow something's missing and parts aren't tied together. A flagrant example of the lack of unity would be a piece that developed an interesting design, but where the application of craft, the finish, the last minute attention to detail was left sloppy. Unity is perhaps an unstated and even unconscious sense of proper blending on the part of the designer. When a piece fits together, when it leaves nothing dangling at loose ends, it then has unity.

Function

To the above principles, I must add the principle of *function*. Function is use. In wood, how can a design be a work of art and be useful at the same time? All wood design is by no means limited to sculpture. As a designer, you need not be afraid of creating something useful. The photographs in the text will prove that design in wood can be artistic and functional: a colonial carved chest, lamps, shop signs, a butter stamp, toys, weather

Mask (Kifwebe), Congo (Democratic Republic): Songe. (far right) 17¾″ high; painted wood. Repetition of line suggesting rhythm almost makes this mask dance by itself. The mask is carved with the addition of veiner-like grooves of texture to create the surface lines. Photo courtesy of The Museum of Primitive Art.

Arrow weathervane, early nineteenth century woodcarving. (right) 30½″ long. Repetition of design line at the feather point from large to small creates the feeling of forward movement. Photo by Einars J. Mengis; courtesy Shelburne Museum, Inc.

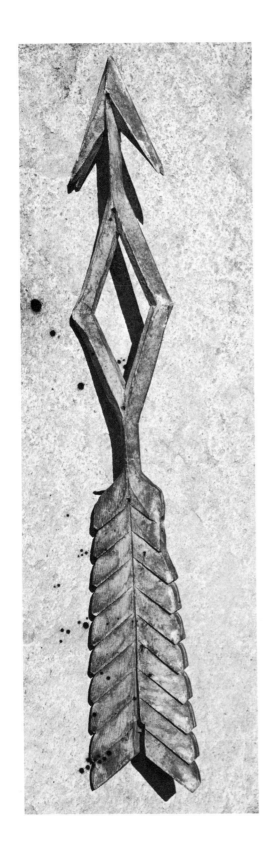

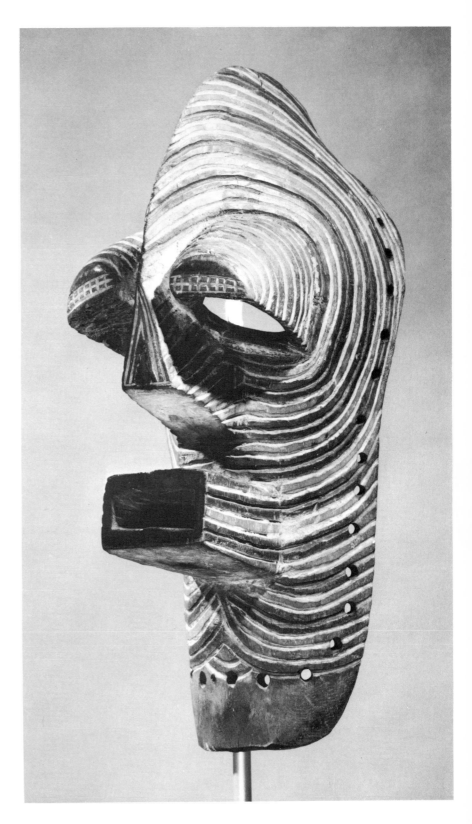

Butter stamp with strawberry, chip carved with contrast in design, accomplished through concentrated detail. Photo by Einars J. Mengis; courtesy Shelburne Museum, Inc.

Bowl by Jerry Glaser. Exotic wood. An example of contrast in texture. The bowl was turned on a lathe in two operations. First, the outside was turned to the approximate shape and then the block was turned around in the lathe and finished on the inside. Texture was added later with hand tools. Photo courtesy The American Craftsman's Council and the artist.

vanes, a wig stand, a music stand, paneling, a granary door, a primitive bench, a contemporary chair, religious symbols, a primitive house post, a bowl, and a baby's cradle. All of these items illustrated in this book were designed from wood, and all have use beyond their artistic value. Primitive and early American folk art were almost exclusively functional. These designers were practical people who combined tasteful art with function. Art for art's sake alone in wood is almost impossible to find among early pieces.

As a designer concerned with function, you might want to consider some questions when you plan your design: will the design compliment its surroundings? Will it do the job I intended? Will it hold up under use? Can it make life more gracious for its consumer? Making a statement that is well designed and functional is one of the most difficult challenges to any artist. Wendell Castle, I think, does just this with his dining room illustrated on page 86. He doesn't simply build a chair, but he gives the consumer a piece of *sculpture* to sit in, something that may enrich the consumer's life.

The planning stage

Design *is* the planning stage. If the design, as conceived by the designer, is unsuccessful, the execution of competent skills matters little. A well planned design radiates a disciplined intent, it does what its creator intended it to do. When I was a lad, I had a neighbor who built a boat in his basement. After he completed the boat, he found he couldn't get it out of the basement. He'd overlooked one obvious detail: planning ahead. Design requires that the designer project his ideas ahead to the finished piece.

Begin simply. Simplicity is not a synonym for incompetency. Simplicity in statement is the goal for every artist; to say something uncluttered. Fussy detail is not the key to successful design. Keep the flow of your design headed in one direction, without interrupting the design for doodles,

and all manner of gimcracks. The repeated intent of this text is to prove to you visually that simplicity reigns as the unequaled giant in art.

Planning your design

Any given design begins first with an idea, and then progresses more or less systematically toward a finished piece. A pattern, paper sketch, or at least a clay model, is, for most people, the smoothest transition in building from an idea to a living three dimensional form. If you prefer sketching directly onto wood without working up something pre-planned, ahead of time, this is possible, although I don't recommend it. Sketching directly onto wood is likely to choke the imagination and produce marks on the wood surface. Because you are sketching, and not exact, these marks may have to be erased or sanded from the finished piece. My recommendation is to first work up a paper sketch of the design, then if you're still curious about its dimensional proportions, work it up in clay, and finally convert the design into a paper pattern.

Spontaneous discovery is one of the most exciting elements of design. Even though your plans are worked out on paper, you should leave plenty of mental room for discovery on the block. Discovery is the element of surprise, of finding something new you hadn't expected after once beginning the process of reduction.

A paper sketch should attack the design from as many planes (front, sides, rear, top, and base) as are necessary to give you a feeling of directed confidence. You need not be fanatically exacting, but generally the more you plan, the less likely you'll goof. A minimum sketch should at least work up the silhouette and, if possible, plan those areas of texture, light, and shadow that will eventually appear on the finished piece. The type of sketch paper used is unimportant since the wood, not the paper, is the subject of your immediate efforts.

If you do try working the design up in modeling clay, you'll give visual reality to the dimension of mass. The most practical clay is the non-hardening

41

42

43

44

45

Baker table by Wendell Castle, 1966. (left) laminated White Oak. Table surface to ceiling: 7′6″; table surface size: 8′ x 6′; weight 800 lbs. Unit consists of two benches and four chairs (two chairs not pictured). The expert design of the chairs and benches elevates them to sculptured furniture. Photo by Charles A. Arnold, Jr.; courtesy of the artist. Collection Mr. and Mrs. Douglas Baker.

Figure 41 *Sketch out your design on a sheet of paper.*

Figure 42 *Draw equidistant horizontal lines across the sheet of paper.*

Figure 43 *Draw equidistant vertical lines across the paper so that the sheet is squared.*

Figure 44 *Now square up a larger sheet of paper, marking the same number of squares on the larger sheet as you had drawn on the smaller.*

Figure 45 *Redraw your sketch in the larger proportion.*

variety (normally called plastiline) that is both pliable and can be reused. Milton Bradley Company, for example, manufactures an inexpensive *Clayrite* non-hardening plastic clay which serves the purpose. Most art suppliers handle non-hardening clay in small quantities. A clay model doesn't have to be life size, but just large enough for visual study purposes.

Whether you sketch directly on the block, use sketch studies, or indulge in clay is a matter of personal preference. Whichever method you do use, plan ahead. Changes should come in planning; not on the block. And try criticizing yourself. Self-criticism is an excellent discipline that squelches intoxication before it occurs. A great danger to any artist is to imbibe his own ideas without looking at them critically.

Arranging your pattern on the block

Before transferring your pattern to the wood block, you should give careful consideration to grain figure, physical strength potential, and any projections that might extend out from the body of the work. The grain figure in the wood can, as we have seen, vividly enhance the statement. Try to make that grain figure work as an integral part of your design. Arrange your pattern on the block so as to squeeze every available ounce of character from the wood. On projections (parts that extend out from the body of the work), the grain should run *with* the length of projection for added physical strength. If the projection is thin—an arm or leg, for example—it may break off under the pressure of your tool. Arranging your pattern on the block to gain the inherent strength available in the wood fiber is excellent insurance against breaks.

While on the subject of projections, let me ad-

Rhythm by the author. 18″ high; Pine. Carved in the round with an X-Acto knife, stained Nutmeg, and finished with three coats of satin varnish. The base was flared and tapered to blend naturally with the design lines. Photo by Dave Congalton.

vise you to allow extra wood for them in your pattern, especially if you cut your outline with a bandsaw. If you don't allow extra wood, you may run short. It's much easier to remove excess wood than to add wood if you misjudge.

Transferring your pattern

You can transfer your pattern to the block by either tracing with non-smear carbon paper, or by covering the back of your pattern with graphite from a soft lead pencil. You can lay your sketch right onto the block, go over the lines lightly, and thus make a direct transfer. Don't press too hard when tracing or the pencil lead may dent the wood more than you had planned. On very large designs, you may have to divide your block into lightly drawn dimensional squares and sketch directly from dimensional squares drawn on the pattern. I'll explain how.

Enlarging and reducing the pattern

If you choose not to sketch to the size of the given block, you'll either have to enlarge or reduce the sketch to make the pattern. If the block is larger than your paper sketch, you'll have to enlarge your sketch to make a pattern; if the block is smaller than your sketch, you'll have to reduce your sketch. But first, before you begin, measure the height, width, and depth of your block. If you don't use the entire block, then measure just the height, width, and depth of that portion of the block you do plan to use.

To enlarge or reduce your sketch, use the old master system of squaring up. You begin by taking your preliminary drawing for your pattern and ruling one-inch squares over the entire page. You then cut a second sheet of paper to the exact size of your block and rule this sheet up with the same number of squares as appear in the original drawing or pattern; naturally, the squares in the second sheet will be either larger or smaller than the squares on the first sheet, depending upon whether you are enlarging or reducing. This procedure just takes some simple elementary arithmetic. You then look at each square in your original drawing or pattern and transfer the lines within this square to the corresponding square on the second sheet to which you are enlarging or reducing your design. (Study Figures 41–45.) The value of this method is simply that it breaks up the original drawing or pattern into bite-size portions which are easier to visualize when you're transferring lines to a larger or smaller sheet.

After you have enlarged or reduced your design to actual size, you transfer the pattern directly to the block as described earlier. And don't forget to repeat this procedure for the various views of the design that appear on all sides of the block.

5 / Techniques

Techniques are the means by which you bring your design into being; you get away from the sketch pad, onto the block, and channel your energy into creating a three dimensional form. Using techniques means applying your tools to a given piece of wood in one of several ways. The techniques offered in this chapter include *relief* carving, *incised* carving, *chip* carving, *direct* carving in the round, *pierced* carving, construction, lamination, and bending. The chapter also includes a discussion of doweling to add detached parts, gluing, and suggestions on combining medium and technique within the same piece.

Approaching the gray area

When a flat paper sketch is transformed into a three dimensional wood form, the designer may experience a momentary period of panic, or loss of direction. The beginning wood designer, before tackling his first piece, will find it reassuring to know that this temporary blind spot of direction happens even to the professional. What often happens is that, as a designer, you're attempting to give a full three dimensional form to what has otherwise been only an idea on a flat, two dimensional paper sketch. Your task is to add the third dimension of depth, and for a short period—while reducing a block to its final form—you may experience a loss of direction, as if you were groping around in a dark room, tentatively feeling your way inch-by-inch.

This momentary blindness is sometimes called the "gray" area in transforming two dimensions into three. On paper, the dimension of depth is not physically present. Once you progress to the point where the design assumes its full three dimensions, your work evolves somewhat by instinct, at least for a short period, until you begin to see your way. When you experience the "gray" area (and you will), I suggest you rely on your eyes and instinct rather than on the paper sketch, itself. With practice, you will learn to approach the gray area with greater courage and direction.

Anatomy of silence by Jules Engel. 16½″ x 13″; painted black wood. Contrasting horizontal and vertical lines in the piece suggest the static sense of silence. The black painted surface enhances the silence by the feeling of night calm. Photo courtesy Ruth White Gallery.

Selecting a technique

The studies on pages 92, 93, 94, 95, 96, and 97, using the identical design of a simple duckling, illustrate the techniques of relief carving, relief carving in the half round, incised carving, chip carving, carving in the round, and the combination of techniques, where an outline is cut to suggest depth, and the duckling is finished with oil colors. These studies were undertaken to point out visually that using the same design—a duckling—but using different techniques, can produce varied results.

In these examples, the play of light and shadow are unique in each piece because of technique. In *Duckling in Oil*, color, and the outline of depth make the statement. *Duckling in the Round* adds the full dimension of depth because the figure may be viewed from all sides. This same duckling could equally have been approached through the additional techniques of construction, lamination, pierced carving, and bent wood. And in addition, any one, or all, of the techniques might have been combined on the same piece.

The point here is that each technique—if it's not combined with other techniques—produces a result of its own. The visual result of the *Duckling in the Round* is entirely different from each of the other ducklings. With which technique do you attack your design? You must answer this question with each new design.

Before deciding to specialize as a constructionist, a chip carver, or a sculptor in the round, find out for yourself what each technique has to offer in releasing the wheels of your imagination. As a similar exercise, I suggest that you try the same series of technique studies on a design of your own. Play around a bit and familiarize yourself with each of the many ways to carry out your de-

Duckling in oil by the author. Duckling 20″ high. Outlined with a veiner on a clear Pine board, and painted with oils mixed with varnish. Background stained fruitwood. Applied frame added from ¼″ thick x 1″ wide strips of clear Pine. Photo by Dave Congalton.

sign. Only then will you have a full feeling of how to express your ideas in wood. And only then, after you've tried *all* the techniques at least once, can you specialize in the area that is most satisfying to you. If you don't open all the doors, you'll never know what's inside.

The man who suggests that one technique is inherently more artful than another is merely playing word games; one technique may be his particular pot of soup, but it's no more or less a legitimate means of making a statement than another technique. Don't be afraid of being branded "crafty" if you chip carve. I've heard it argued that chip carving is merely a lower form of doodling. That self-made critic probably never tried it himself. If the design and the technique make a strong and original statement—regardless of what technique you've selected—you've done your best. And besides, nothing's really wrong with being branded "crafty." In my dictionary, *crafty* means skillful and ingenious, not such a difficult "brand" to live with after all.

At this point, many books would offer specific follow-the-number projects on each technique, such as an opening statement like: "All right now readers, in today's lesson we'll all pick up our tools and carve a bumble bee in relief." This approach is apparently justified by an author in order to develop the skill of his reader. Skill or competence in craft certainly doesn't come from imposing ideas, especially beginnings, on a reader. I don't buy this approach and will therefore skip it entirely.

At some point my reader must make his own break from the white page. To impose a specific elementary design project only delays this process. And besides, I'm assuming my contemporary reader is a very bright and inventive human being if he's left to discover by himself. I shudder at the

Duckling in relief by the author. Duckling 20″ high; Pine. Outline cut with a chisel and background removed with a gouge. A natural 1″ border was left at surface level to provide a frame. Piece was stained fruitwood and shaded. Photo by Dave Congalton.

thought of imposing any limitations on your ideas when, potentially, freedom to express and discover is yours; and woe to me if I inhibit your beginning! A brief and simple discussion of each technique will follow. I believe you'll see the light. Hopefully it shines brightly.

Relief carving

In the most familiar sort of relief carving, the motif is part of a flat surface which is cut back so that the motif is elevated, projecting up and away from a plain background. Light and shadow play an important role in relief carving: the deeper the relief (the higher it rises above the flat surface), the more pronounced will be the contrast between motif and background. A shallow relief will not capture the same degree of light and shadow contrast captured on a deep relief.

In the simplest method of relief carving, the background is partially cut away—literally *lowered* —leaving the motif at the original surface level of the block of wood. In this instance, depending upon the lines of the motif, either a gouge or a chisel is used first to outline the motif with a stop cut. The background is then removed to a specified, pre-planned depth with a gouge, leaving a clean, pronounced outline around the edge of the motif. The motif can then be given additional texturing for light and shadow by varying its depth with a gouge, or by rounding or beveling the edges of the outline. In *Duckling in Relief*, the background was removed to a depth of ¾ inch, and one surface line was added with a veiner for detail of the wing line. Several other examples of this type of relief carving are included in the text.

In another type of relief, the motif is carved in

Duckling in the half round by the author. Duckling 20″ high. Carved in the half round from a 4″ thick piece of clear Pine after first being sawed in profile on a band saw. The duckling was mounted to a weathered barn board in relief by wood screws from the back. Brass ring added for hanging. Photo by Dave Congalton.

the half round, and later applied, or mounted to a plain background. (See *Duckling in the Half Round* on page 94.) In this illustration, the duckling was attached to a weathered panel by wood screws inserted from the back. In both these styles of relief, the background is *recessed*, that is, lower than the motif.

As indicated above, many relief carvings are combined with other techniques. For example, the background can be textured with gouge strokes, broken up into a pattern of veiner lines, or even chip patterns.

Generally, your relief will come across stronger when the contrast of surface depth—between the recessed background and the motif itself—is left uncluttered with extra ornamentation. This is not to say that chip cuts on a relief are in bad taste, but only to point out that the strength of the contrasting surface depths created by relief will be greatly reduced by ornamentation. The whole point of relief is to create light and shadow contrast, therefore the more visually pronounced your depth contrast is, the greater will be the dimensional effect. On the *Duckling in Relief*, I could very well have applied veiner lines to the duckling for each feather, but I would have then destroyed the effect of relief. With feather lines, the duckling may have been more precise in detail, but it would also have been much busier visually. I chose to leave the duckling plain in order to emphasize the contrast in surface depth. With a familiar figure like a duckling, feathers seem to be implied anyway.

Incised carving

To incise is to cut into the surface of wood. On an incised carving the entire motif is recessed

Duckling incised by the author. Duckling 20″ high. Incised ¾″ into a 1″ thick piece of clear Pine by first making an outline with a chisel and then removing excess wood with a gouge. Wing and tail line added with a veiner. Breadboard framing method cut with a table saw. Piece was stained fruitwood and shaded. Photo by Dave Congalton.

95

below the original wood surface, just the opposite from relief. In *Duckling Incised* illustrated on page 95, the entire duckling was incised (recessed) to a depth of ¾ inch below the surrounding surface. Incising is done in the same manner as relief: one tool cuts an outline with a stop cut, and a second tool removes the wood to form a clean, pronounced outline. As in relief, the motif, once recessed, can then be textured. And, as in relief, the motif is visually stronger if the background is left undisturbed.

Chip carving

Chip carving is made with a series of precise geometric cuts; the designer works with planes and, when seen together, the cuts make a total statement (see *Duckling Chip Carved* to the left). The motif on a chip carving is divided into a flowing series of individual cuts or chips; each chip having its own identity, but being a part of the whole. The angle of the planes is determined beforehand and is worked out on the paper pattern. The ridges (crisp edges) of each chip remain distinct in order to distinguish one chip from another, and to create the lines of the total design. There is a strong contrast of shadow and light in chip carving because of the interplay of geometric planes.

Any combination of stop cuts, or stop and slice cuts will produce a chip. The gouge, chisel, veiner, parting tool, and the knife may be used separately, or in combination to make a chip. It's important in chip carving to make clean, distinct, and deep chips in order to avoid design ambiguity. To do this, each chip must meet the next evenly. Chip cuts can be angled toward an inverted pyramidal center, or they can have a flat base with vertical

Duckling chip carved by the author. Duckling 20″ high. Chip carved into a 1″ thick piece of clear Pine, stained fruitwood, and shaded with heavy and light applications of stain wiped with a cloth. Photo by Dave Congalton.

sides. End cuts can either be angled or vertical. It's also important to arrange your pattern on the block so that the flow of the cuts (the length of the cuts), runs *with* the grain. Try a practice board, preferably soft wood, and experiment for yourself. Figures 46 and 47 give some examples of a few chips made with a chisel and gouge.

After the design is completed into a series of chips, the chips can be smoothed with sandpaper, or with the abrasive bit on a motor tool to cover mistakes and hack marks, but don't smooth the chips to the point where they become soft and indistinct. If a ridge from one of the chips breaks off, save it and glue it back in place when you're through. Instead of gluing a ridge back, you can also cover the break in a ridge by carefully scooping the broken ridge down to the depth of the break. The larger cuts in *Duckling Chip Carved* were recessed ½ inch below the original surface, and were cut with an X-Acto knife blade.

A chip carving need not be thought of as only surface decoration or as a means of filling up blank surface area with a "folksy" arrangement of cuts. Cuts can suggest and carry out rhythm, emphasis, and balance. Chip cuts, whether applied to relief, incised designs, or carving in the round, should work with, and strengthen the total statement. I don't recommend buying plates, bowls, and boxes to decorate with chip carving unless you do this only for an exercise. I would much prefer that you make the entire object on which the cuts appear. Chip cuts should work with the total design.

Direct carving in the round

The distinguishing feature of carving in the round is that the design is completely three dimensional;

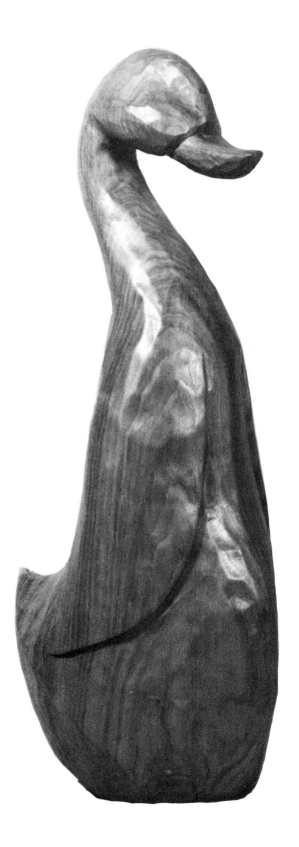

Duckling in the round by the author. 20″ high; Butternut. Design carved in the full round with a gouge and mallet after first being sawed in profile on a band saw. Sanded to leave a light texture and finished natural with three coats of satin finish varnish, lightly sanded between coats. Photo by Dave Congalton.

Figure 46 *A few sample chip cuts made with a chisel; the chisel adapts itself best to precise, straight-edged cuts.*

Figure 47 *A few sample chip cuts made with a gouge; the gouge works best with curved chip cuts, or can be combined with the chisel for a variety of effects.*

Acrobats by the author. 14″ long x 10″ high; pierced
carving, Black Walnut figures mounted on Bird's-eye
Maple base. Figures cut from a single piece of Walnut
planed to ½″ thick, then beveled with a wood rasp,
and finished natural. Photo by Dave Congalton.

100

it is viewed from all sides. The line no longer has a separate existence (see *Duckling in the Round* on page 97). It now either represents the junction of two planes, or it exists as the outline contour or outer edge of the object in space. When designing a three dimensional sculpture, it's important to remember that the object is meant to be viewed from all positions: front, back, top, sides, and base.

Too many designers approach three dimensional carving from the wrong end. They work up a statement that looks squeezed into the block, as if they had first selected a block and then felt obligated to fill every square inch of available space with design. The result of this approach is obvious to the trained eye; the piece very often is crouched, bent, or twisted into a position that communicates a lack of freedom. I strongly suggest that you give your design elbow room on the block, unless you deliberately mean to crowd it for effect. Don't try to squeeze your figure into a head bent, kneeling, tummy-hugging fetal position because you have only a small piece of wood. Give the design freedom on the block. One way to avoid squeezing is by working up your design first—to the size you want—and then get a block that will fit your design. If you begin *first* with a block, then conceive a design that will fit into the block, you very well may crowd yourself. Design to size first, and then seek out the block to fit your design.

Figures 48 to 52 illustrate how a design in the round is reduced to its final form. This piece was cut in outline on a bandsaw (see Figure 49), and elbow room was left between the actual line of the figure and the line of the saw cut. The opening between the arms and body was first drilled with a bit large enough so that the bandsaw blade could be inserted in the hole. The bandsaw blade was then inserted into the hole, and the opening was cut. The figure was arranged on the block in such a way that the grain flow could both accent the lines of the figure, and add strength to the thin arms.

With each step of removing excess wood, the

Figure 48 *Pattern is drawn on the block to take advantage of grain flow. Care should be taken to see that the front and side views line up evenly (see dotted lines at neck, shoulders, waist, knees, and ankles above).*

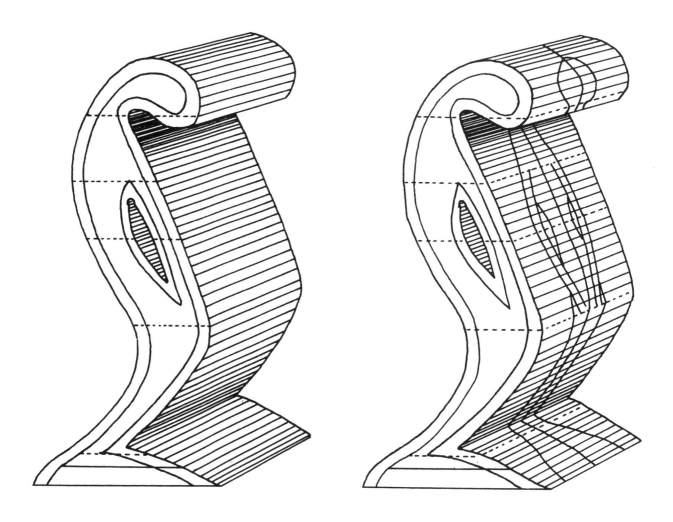

Figure 49 *Profile cut on band saw, leaving extra room beyond the actual design line. The center arm hole was cut on a band saw after first drilling a hole large enough to hold the blade.*

Figure 50 *After the profile is cut, the front view is again re-established using the same guidelines (dotted lines).*

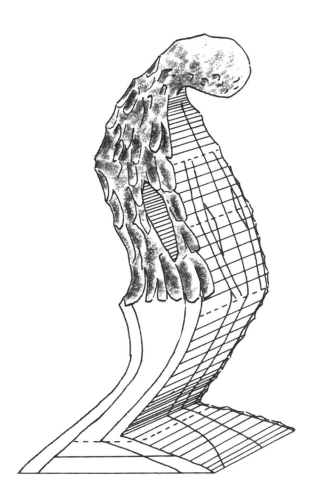

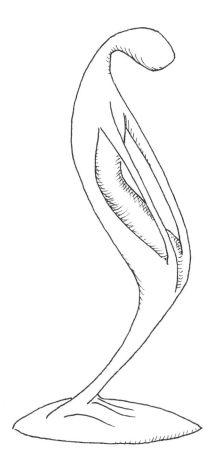

Figure 51 *Reduction with the tool begins.*

Figure 52 *The finished piece.*

surface of the block was divided into sections with pencil markings (dotted lines shown in Figure 49) on each of the four long sides of the wood, in order to keep track of proportion. This gives the designer a visual reference point to compare planes: the neck, chest, waist, knees, and ankles on the figure illustrated. You can see how this is helpful by noticing (in the illustration) that the thinnest ankle line on the side view is *not* the thinnest point on the front view. The ankle is somewhat oval at its narrowest point, being thinner when viewed from the front than when viewed from the side. True or exact dimensional proportion, therefore, cannot be planned ahead of time until the block is reduced in this manner. After you've done a number of pieces, proportion will become a matter of instinct and you won't have to go through all of these careful reduction procedures. But if you're in doubt, this method might build up self-confidence.

A three dimensional carving in the round can be reduced to its final form with a variety of tools. The tools used will depend upon the size of the design and the tools available to you. My rule of thumb is to use whichever tools feel most comfortable on the block and which will reduce the figure with the least investment of time.

Pierced carving

In pierced carving, all background is completely removed by a pattern of openings *around* and *through* the wood to leave the design silhouetted against space. In other words, in pierced carving, external and internal space is used to create the lines of design. Pierced carving can be either in the full round or simply approached to form a silhouette in relief, to be seen only from the front. The concern in pierced carving is to let in *negative space*, space within the design, as well as around it.

Pierced carving, mounted on panels, is a familiar technique used on religious motifs, and was used extensively in fifteenth, sixteenth, and seventeenth century furniture carving, especially on chairs and chests. It is sometimes called fretwork. By letting light in through openings, negative space creates the silhouette. I prefer finishing a design of pierced carving on all sides, so that even if it's mounted against a panel, or on a wall, it visually implies three dimensions.

Acrobats on page 100 illustrates a free standing example of pierced carving. This study was made from a single piece of Walnut planed to ½ inch thick, and mounted on a base of Bird's-eye Maple. I cut the openings with a bandsaw, first drilling a hole in each space to admit the width of the saw blade. All sides of the piece were then reduced to proportions with an X-Acto knife, rasp, riffler, and sandpaper.

When experimenting with pierced carving, I suggest you use hard wood. I tried this same piece on a number of other woods before settling on Walnut. With such large areas of open space, I found that soft wood warped easily, and lacked the fiber strength to support the piece when it was being reduced to dimensional proportions.

The mobile illustrated on page 54 is another example of pierced work. The openings of the mobile provide a kinetic play of light between interacting parts. This piece was made from lightweight Masonite. It has a flat surface ¼ inch thick and was not cut to proportion.

Construction

A construction in wood is a design where the arrangement and connection of *separate* parts, or groups of separate parts, form a statement. A construction can be done either in the full round or in relief, as when mounted against a wall. Unlike carving in the round, where wood is removed, a wood construction is *built*; separate parts are attached to each other to form a whole. The assemblage of parts may be left as natural forms, shaped by machine, or shaped with hand tools.

Individual parts can be assembled in a number of ways, depending upon the designer's preference and the particular joining problems at hand. Parts

Untitled, wood frame construction by Sol Lewitt, 1966, painted white. The outside frame is 84" x 84" x 84"; the inside frame 30" x 30" x 30". Photo courtesy Dwan Gallery.

Last supper by Mario Ceroli, 1965. (left) Laminated shipping crates used as material for the cut-out figures. 58″ x 88″ x 27″. Mr. Ceroli very often employs the use of hinged pieces (small cupboard hinges) in order to add movement to his designs by stretching and even changing their positions. Photo courtesy Bonino Gallery.

Black sleeping nude by Anne Arnold, 1966. (above) 6′ long. This piece was constructed from two-inch Pine planks sawed with a Sawzall, doweled, and then glued. The figure is painted black and mounted horizontally on two white-painted Pine planks. Photo courtesy Fischbach Gallery.

may be glued, doweled, hinged, dove-tailed by mortice and tenon (the way in which corners are attached in drawers), nailed, or assembled with wood screws. For example, Mario Ceroli, a young Italian sculptor, uses ordinary cupboard door hinges to join his parts. His constructions then move, stretch, and flex.

Constructions can be built from natural wood forms, plywood, solid wood pieces, toothpicks, or even—as in the case of Mr. Ceroli's work (illustrated on page 106)—out of discarded shipping crates. There's no limit to the availability of material for a wood construction if you use your imagination.

Louise Nevelson, one of the deans of contemporary wood construction (see *Night Zag IV* on page 116) creates an environment of parts with her constructions. Her free standing assemblage is so large that it surrounds the viewer; the viewer is consumed by the design and identifies with it. A Nevelson construction might include table legs, apple boxes, stair rungs, and discarded bits of geometric scraps.

Anne Arnold's piece (*Black Sleeping Nude* on page 107) was constructed from two-inch Pine planks. The parts were doweled and then glued. Shaping was added to suggest proportion. On her animal figures, Miss Arnold uses slab wood and preserves the swelling, organic shape of the original tree to reveal the form within a controlled cut-out contour.

Frame construction is another form of assemblage. With this type of construction, the designer builds a statement within a framework. The piece almost seems to assume the form of a rib cage, where the eye is concerned with what's inside holding the design together. Students of architecture often use frame construction to gain insight into stress and support in wood. Sol Lewitt's piece on page 105 uses frame construction as a clear statement rather than as a study. Still another approach to construction is through geometric solids, as in the case of Richard Randell's *Big Zero* on page 76.

Lamination

Lamination is the process of sandwiching layers of wood together to produce volume, line, or a combination of both. Every lamination creates an additional line where you can actually see the two layers of wood placed together. If the designer is primarily interested in gaining wood volume through lamination, he may prefer to place his layers together to gain physical strength, rather than to accent grain flow. If he wanted only the maximum strength (as was the case in George Sugarman's painted *Bardana* on the facing page), he would laminate each layer of wood so that the direction of the grain would be at a right angle to the preceding layer. This method of lamination for strength reduces the possibility of expansion and contraction between layers and in the over-all piece.

If, on the other hand, the designer is concerned with line (making use of the lines created by sandwiching layers), he would arrange his layers to gain the most from the grain figure, and from the lines of lamination. In this instance, he would probably arrange his layers together so that when laminated, all the grains ran in the same direction. Mike Nevelson's *Victory At Sea* on page 110, made from layers of Pine, was laminated with the grains and lamination lines arranged to gain horizontal emphasis.

Jack Squier's *Flat Creature IV* on page 111, made from Mahogany, was laminated in layers to gain both volume and line.

The way in which you arrange the layers of grain flow (parallel or perpendicular) will therefore accent the inherent lines of the design. Combinations of wood species (tones of dark and light) may be laminated to take advantage of natural grain and textural differences between woods.

Layers may be laminated with glue by covering both surfaces with a woodworking glue, pressing them together, and then clamping them tightly with C clamps. Wood screws can be used to laminate if the head of the screw is recessed *below* the outer surface and then filled over with wood filler

Bardana by George Sugarman. 12′ long x 8′ high x 5′
wide; laminated wood. Mr. Sugarman thinks of wood
as a substance for volume in sculpture; his
laminations are arranged for strength. Pieces were cut
in profile and shaped with belt and disk sanders. Color
here works; the sequence of events is alive with energy
created by color and shape. The red-painted, horizontal
fan-like, radiating center lines suddenly stop the flow.
Photo courtesy Fischbach Gallery.

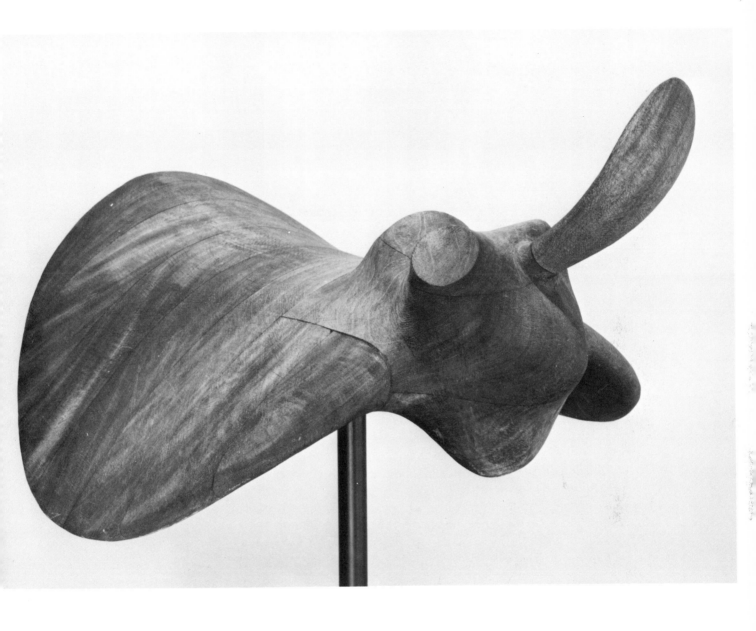

Victory at sea by Mike Nevelson. (left) 8 feet high; laminated Pine. Lamination here creates strength of horizontal line; the calm that follows battle. Photo courtesy of the artist.

Flat creature IV by Jack Squier, 1963. (above) 35″ long; laminated Mahogany. Lamination here gains both line and volume. Photo courtesy Landau-Alan Gallery.

to cover the screw head. Or wood screws can be used on inner layers and glue on the final exterior surface layer. Recessed nails can be used to laminate in the same manner as with wood screws, although generally they won't hold as well as wood screws.

Doweling is still another means of holding layers together; the dowel runs through all layers. First drill a hole through the layers and then glue the dowel in place as the holding device. Even interlocking parts, as in *Appendicular Puzzle*, by William Keyser on page 113, may be used as the device to hold layers of wood together. On heavy or thick chunks of wood, lag bolts (purchased from a hardware store) will hold layers together. These can be left either with bolt heads exposed (if you have a reason for doing so), or the heads can be recessed below the exposed surface (as with wood screws) and filled over with wood filler or a dowel end.

Lamination in wood to gain volume has been around a long time. Early American folk artists used the laminated technique on shop signs, ship figureheads, circus pieces, and more especially on the carved eagles passed down for preservation in museums. These pieces were so large that the only way to obtain large enough chunks of wood was to sandwich layers of wood together. However, grain figure, texture, and tone difference have been exploited mainly by the contemporary designer.

Bending

Bending is the process of producing sharp curvature in wood members to preserve the flow of grain. If the curved member on a design had been cut on a bandsaw—cut to the arc of the curve rather than bent—the grain flow would run out along the curved surface rather than continue to flow with the curvature of the member. Bending is therefore decorative in that it preserves the natural beauty of grain and holds it within the member rather than allowing it to run out, as in the case of sawing a curve. I won't engage in academic discussions of whether a bent member is stronger than a cut curve because one needs a given situation each time in order to make a choice. The primary advantage in bending—and a great one, it seems to me—is that the beauty in grain figure is kept intact.

Bending, in wood design, is used particularly on functional pieces, usually furniture, and it is used more for beauty than for strength. The bent member may be either solid or laminated in layers. In lamination, the adjoining grain flow may be parallel or, when added strength is needed, may be perpendicular (laminations at right angles). Laminations may be either separately bent and then glued, or glued first and then bent. In the sections ahead, both procedures will be outlined.

Hard wood is better for bending than soft wood, especially such hard woods as Elm, Oak, Beech, Birch, Ash, Hickory, Maple, and Mahogany. A bent member should have an even grain flow, and should be free of knots or wild grain interruption.

Freshly cut green wood is unsuitable for bending, as is wood that is corky dry. It's difficult to stabilize a bend in green wood; and wood that is too dry (that looks corky in appearance) requires lengthy soaking beforehand to bring it to a plastic, or flexible state. If you avoid the two extremes, you should come up with a suitable material.

To bend wood in a studio situation, the wood should first be soaked in hot water, as near to the steaming point as possible. A large washtub, sink, bathtub, or even shower stall can serve the purpose. The plastic, or flexible point of wood varies with each species, and according to the moisture content in the wood before the soaking. Trial and error on a given piece is the only guideline I can offer. If it bends where you want it to bend, the wood is then ready.

When the moisture content is great enough for bending, the piece should be quickly clamped to a pre-shaped wooden form, preferably hard wood cut with a bandsaw to the exact curvature desired. The piece to be bent is forced against the pre-shaped form by tightening clamps, a little at a time, evenly along the length of the bend. A buffer of leather, cork, or a thin wood chip between the clamp and the bent piece will prevent the clamp jaw from denting the wood.

While still clamped to the form, the piece of wood should dry to the approximate weight and texture appearance as was present before it was soaked. When the bent member is dry, the clamps can be removed, and the curvature should remain fixed. If it pops back a little, you may have to repeat the process and increase the curvature of the form to allow for the loss.

The process of bending laminated pieces after they are glued is similar to that of bending solid pieces of wood. The glue used in lamination should be able to withstand the soaking process. When you laminate several wood pieces intended for bending, take care to laminate the two pieces with the straightest, or least interrupted grain figures on the two exposed surfaces; these two pieces (the top piece and the bottom piece in the lamination) will show and withstand the most stress. The very best piece, the piece with the least interruption in grain figure, should be reserved for the *inside* of the bend because it has to curve the most. For further information on bending, write for the Forest Products Laboratory Handbook #72, mentioned in the chapter on wood.

Doweling and attaching parts

Dowels, screws, nails, and bolts are used on carving in the round, construction, and lamination to increase wood volume. The particular problem at hand and the effect you want to gain will dictate which of the items to use. No one

Appendicular puzzle by William A. Keyser, Jr. 10″ x 16″ x 28″ high; Cherry construction. Individual pieces held together by pins and wedges; no glue. The piece is a knock-down (it comes apart). The lower two-thirds is sanded smooth; the upper one-third is textured rough. Photo courtesy of the artist.

method is any more or less artful than another, as long as it does the job it was intended to do. Generally speaking, nails, screws, dowels, and even glue can be used on lighter weight designs where there is a minimum of stress on the joined parts. Splinters that might occur by accident can also be held in place by the same variety of items. Lag bolts can be used on very large pieces and on designs with massive weight. Unless you have a particular reason to expose nails, screws, and bolts, they should be recessed below the exposed wood surface, and then filled over with wood filler, or with a dowel end. Dowels can be left exposed to the eye, if you don't mind their appearance. Remember, a dowel end has its own grain figure. Be careful to place the dowel so that the end grain works well with the design.

A dowel is fitted by drilling holes (the same diameter and length as the dowel) into each attached part at the point where the hole on both pieces *sleeves*, or fits over the dowel. The dowel should have a snug fit. A drop of glue in each hole will hold the dowel in place. If the dowel is too loose in the hole, you can either slip a sliver of wood into the hole or drive a small wedge of wood into an exposed dowel end to force apart the dowel fibers. This is the same method used on the handles of hammers and axes.

Gluing

The most important point in gluing is to wipe, or scrape off, all excess glue before the finish is applied. Elmer's Woodworking Glue, for example, will not absorb stain; thus, if glue is left on exposed surfaces, a white blotch will appear on the wood surface, advertising your mistake. Glue is an excellent means of attaching parts as long as you can keep exposed surfaces free of excess, if you've

Hexagon lamp by the author. Base: 22″ high; Pine. Panels were incised with a chisel to a depth of ⅜″. Welded, free form metal panels were glued in place with epoxy. Photo by Dave Congalton.

got the patience to let the glue sit, and if the joint is not exposed to heavy stress.

A variety of wood glues is available from artist suppliers and hardware stores; for example, Weldwood glue, epoxy glue, all-purpose cement, and Elmer's glue. I've experimented with most of them and each of them contains similar qualities, as well as qualities that are unique. For example, Elmer's has an all-purpose cement that can be used on wood. You put two coats on each surface to be joined and let each coat dry before the next is applied. Then the two completely dry coats on each surface are pressed together to create the bond. I cannot recommend one glue over another because the joining problem at hand is different in each case. Generally speaking, Weldwood, epoxy, and Elmer's Woodworking Glue give a strong bond, but must be carefully cleaned up to avoid excess appearing on exposed surfaces. Glue and cement are reasonably inexpensive. I suggest that you experiment with each type to discover the qualities in them that will solve your particular joining problem.

Combining techniques

Any combination of the techniques in this chapter may be applied to the same design. (Heaven forbid that you try them all on the same piece!) You may also try more than one medium on the same piece, as for example, the lamp illustrated on page 114 combines direct carving in the round with welded metal panels on the sides, and *The Palace at 4:00 a.m.* by Alberto Giacometti on page 69 combines several media in one piece.

There are a number of illustrations in the text that combine various media and techniques. There is chip carving on laminated wood in relief, and even chip carved construction. Try to identify these technique and medium combinations for yourself. If you succeed, you've been listening.

Driftwood panel by Stella M. Lowry. 20″ x 6′ high. A construction of found pieces of driftwood cemented with Anchorweld Cement on the reverse side of tempered Masonite. Photo by Vern Chester.

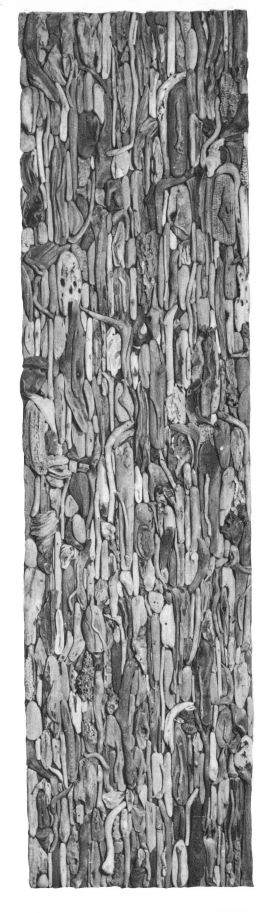

6/Finishing

Night zag IV by Louise Nevelson, 1965. 20 double units; 92½" high with base. Black painted wood and Plexiglas with mirror panels. Mrs. Nevelson creates a total environment in her constructions. In this piece we can see a busy night filled with shadows, reflections, unrest, but yet a feeling of subtle dignity. Her zig-zag base tells you something's going on. The mirror reflections placed against black-painted objects confirm this. Photo courtesy Pace Gallery.

Hold on! You aren't *finished* yet.

Before lugging that design off to the nearest art gallery, it may require some type of finish. Finishing is a technique in itself, and can often improve and extend your statement. It is the fussy part of wood design, and should be executed carefully, in the same manner as a bride checks her appearance in a mirror before attending her wedding. Finishing can be the *pièce de résistance* to the eye. That bride is perfect; every hair is in place, every button buttoned, every strap strapped. She makes an impact by her finish. Drips, drools, and brush hairs left on a completed wood design only advertise sloppiness. It's like that bride attending her wedding with her hair in curlers, slip showing, and one nylon dangling loose for public disapproval.

Finishing then, is the planned, final, and fussy treatment of the design after you've set aside your tools. Planning the finish involves several considerations: surface texture, surface color, and surface durability.

Surface texture may be smoothed by sanding. You may prefer to leave the texture rough by exposing tool marks, or by artificially applying texture with oils and acrylics, as done by artists on canvas. Surface color can be added, highlighted, or enriched through the application of paint and stain. Surface durability can be added by sealing the wood fibers with varnish, shellac, or wax. The application of one given finish may produce more than one result, as for example, a varnish base Walnut stain on Pine will darken the surface color, and seal the wood for durability. In the same manner, red oil paint applied to wood will change the color to red, seal the surface fiber and, if heavy enough in application, will add surface texture to an otherwise smooth piece by heavy layers of brush strokes. This chapter will discuss a number of finishing procedures. Familiarity with finishes, and what they will do, develops with practice.

Almost all finishes, to some degree, seal wood fiber. Sealing reduces expansion and contraction, especially if applied equally to all exposed surfaces: back, front, sides, top, and base. The change in moisture content which causes the expansion and contraction of wood can result in surface cracks and splits. These may never show up, or they might suddenly appear after several months, or even years. Sealing the wood surface reduces the possibility of cracks and splits in a finished piece.

Many designers prefer completing large designs without finish, anticipating the cracks and splits which will add character to the design at some later date. I've even known designers to deliberately expose sculpture directly to the elements in order to force surface cracks. Unless you have this in mind, I suggest you use an applied finish.

Before deciding on a finish, it's important to consider texture, color, and durability. But it's also important to allow the design to speak for itself; see if the lines of your design suggest anything to you in the way of finish. Selection of the right finish can enhance the strength of any statement.

Almost every wood designer has his own recipe for finishing wood, from homemade brews, to commercial products, to laborious, secretive wax applications. Yours will come too, with practice.

Sanding

If you decide on a smooth surface for your design, sanding is the first step in finishing. Sandpaper and steel wool are both abrasives; they remove wood by wearing away the surface. Sandpaper and steel wool are both sold according to the texture of cutting surface: from fine to coarse. The stages of sanding should always progress from coarse to fine.

Sanding can often be very laborious and time consuming, especially if done by hand. Don't quit in the middle. Keep going until the surface reaches the degree of smoothness you had originally intended. A wood design has a surface to be felt. This "feel" can enrich the total impact of your design. Careful sanding pays off.

Hand sanding, whether with sandpaper or steel

wool, should work *with* the wood grain, even on end grain. Sanding across the grain often produces scratches from the grit in the paper. And if you use a vibrating or oscillating sander, you should always hand sand afterwards. An electric sander, especially one that oscillates, will often leave tiny scratched circles on the wood surface. Many times these can't be seen until a finish is applied, and then it's too late. To avoid the scratches, always hand sand after using the electric sander.

When finishing with varnish, shellac, or a varnish base stain, it's also important to sand lightly between coats. Sanding between coats does not apply to wax finishes. A fine grade of steel wool works best for between-coat sanding. This extra bit of effort removes dust flecks, lumps that may have been present in the finish, brush hairs, and provides a lightly textured surface to help the next coat adhere.

Stain

Stain applied to wood may either change the surface color, enrich the grain figure, or highlight areas within a design by shading. If you decide on a stain, staining is the next step after sanding. Stain is applied on raw or unfinished wood. A prepared surface for stain must be free of grease, wax, glue, or any other foreign material. Stain will not penetrate through these materials.

Commercial stain is sold in colors with either an oil or varnish base. An oil base stain leaves a mat texture; the pores of wood fiber remain unsealed. A varnish base stain, on the other hand, both colors and seals the wood. Oil base commercial stains work best for shading, but take longer to dry.

It's also possible to *make* your own stain by first selecting a vehicle—white gas and turpentine are

Geoffrey by Anne Arnold. 40½″ high; painted Pine. The folk-like quality of this free standing piece resembles the simplicity of early American art. Photo courtesy Fischbach Gallery.

Bust of a young woman by William King. (left)
16″ high; Mahogany. Compare this bust with the folk
carved early American wig stand illustrated on page 12.
The similarities are delightful. Although Mr. King
had never seen the wig stand at the Shelburne
Museum, his own interpretation of the figure seems to
be a rebirth of the folk artist's vision. Photo courtesy
Terry Dintenfass Gallery; collection, Judge and Mrs.
Samuel Rosenman.

Little boy by Mike Nevelson. 55″ high. In this piece,
Mr. Nevelson uses the functional form of furniture
as the subject matter for sculpture; the design is
sculpture, not furniture. Furniture is the means by which
he builds the sculpture. Photo courtesy of the artist.

both excellent vehicles—and then adding color. The vehicle carries the color into the wood and then evaporates. Oil paint pigment can be added to either white gas or turpentine to produce the color you want. Strong tea and coffee will also produce color for stain if mixed with *water* as the vehicle.

Every species of wood has its unique natural color and grain texture. It's virtually impossible to predict from the color stated on a can what color will result on a given piece of wood. The same stain may produce a dark reaction on Pine and have no effect on Walnut. For this reason, when buying commercial stains, or even making your own stain, it's essential to try the stain first on a scrap of wood left over from your design, before you apply it to the entire piece.

If you want a uniform stain throughout the design, it's best to brush on the stain and wipe it off with a cloth. Apply the stain evenly, in equal doses, and control the time it remains on the wood. A heavy application left for long periods produces a uniform dark stain. A thin application wiped off quickly produces a uniform light stain. Don't just slop stain all over the piece. Stain should be applied carefully with a soft, absorbent cloth or a brush. Although slopping stain in large doses does produce uniformity, it saturates the wood and makes shading difficult.

Shading and highlighting with stain

A stained piece need not be uniform in tone. The application of stain can be controlled for shading and highlighting. In fact, as I mentioned earlier, I've found oil base stains most suitable for shading.

If you want to produce shadow, texture, or tone differences, you must control the quantity of stain

---

Manhattan theme VIII by Mike Nevelson. 21″ high; doweled Pine. On this piece the artist uses the repetition of vertical lines to suggest dignity in the blend of people and skyscrapers. Photo courtesy of the artist.

applied and the amount of time the stain remains full strength on the wood. Shading with stain works best with a cloth. Light areas are produced by first applying stain evenly and then wiping it off the light areas quickly with a second absorbent cloth. Dark areas are produced by allowing a heavy, full strength application to stand until dry. Even darker areas can be produced by second and third applications, allowing each application to dry thoroughly before the next is applied. The duckling, illustrated on page 96, shows tone differences produced by controlling the application of stain.

When shading with stain, the areas of tone difference should blend gradually without leaving abrupt lines. A dab of turpentine on a cloth will help you blend tone areas.

If a piece contains recessed or raised areas, a brush will help get at hard-to-reach spots. Or you might wrap a cloth around a nail tip, or around any other pointed object to get the same result.

Clear finish

Clear finish makes grain vivid. Varnish is one type of clear finish. A piece that doesn't get much handling can be finished with clear varnish. Varnish is sold according to gloss and varies in texture from mat, to satin, to high gloss. If the piece is to be handled, varnish may wear off. A scratch on a varnished surface will leave a mark.

Linseed oil and Val oil are two other types of clear finish. These two oils are well suited for pieces that *will* be handled. The task of sanding over, and covering a surface scratch on an oil finished piece is much simpler than on a piece finished with varnish. Shellac is still another clear finish. Many designers use shellac as a surface sealer. My own prejudice is that shellac has too much gloss, and is a bit gooey to work with in comparison to varnish.

Clear finish should be applied in coats; one coat builds upon another. A particularly porous wood may require several coats. The color a drop of clear water produces on a piece of raw wood approximates the color the wood will turn when you use a clear finish.

Wax

Wax may be applied directly to raw wood or applied as a final finish over a stained and varnished surface. Beeswax is perhaps the best wax on wood, but it's expensive. It is available in liquid form. Paste waxes, such as household Johnson's Paste Wax, and Carnauba Wax, also work well on wood. Unlike liquid wax, paste wax may clog in surface breaks. It also has a fawn color of its own, so excess should be wiped off. Wax, when buffed with a soft cloth, produces a silky feel to the touch.

Color

Color on wood crosses into the medium of painting, where a whole new set of values apply. Without going into color charts, and the relationships between colors, it's sufficient to say that color is more than a decoration. Louise Nevelson (see page 116), uses black to suggest mystery, shadow, and dawns, dusks, and in-between places. George Sugarman (see page 109), uses color to pull a piece along, stretch it out, stop it, or even expand and contract it. His color arrangement goes beyond decoration. It works. It makes the eye move. Colors are positioned so that the eye is pushed in the direction intended by the sculptor. Color, then, can make its own statement. But color also hides the natural beauty of wood, an aspect you should bear in mind when you consider using it. The choice of finish is yours.

Watercolor. Watercolor on porous wood—such as Pine—leaves a soft, dye-like appearance; it allows the wood grain to show through the color. Watercolors are unsuitable for hard wood and wood with a dark natural color. Hard wood does not easily absorb watercolor and, on dark wood, watercolors will not show up. Working with watercolor on porous wood requires that you allow one color to completely dry before applying another, otherwise the two colors will fray into each other. Normally you don't apply water on wood, but with watercolors, the penetration is negligible and the water acts as the vehicle for the color and then quickly evaporates.

Oil color. Oil color can be used directly on wood, or mixed with turpentine and varnish to speed drying time and provide durability. (Varnish acts as a hardener; turpentine a thinner.) Texture, on a smooth surface, can be built up with layers of oil applied with a brush. A quick drying varnish mixed with oil will speed up the building of layers by forcing the oil to dry.

Other colors. Acrylic colors, or synthetics as they're sometimes called, can also be used on wood. Many designers prefer acrylics because the colors are said to be more vivid, dry more quickly, and, hopefully, will outlast oil. Colored enamels may also be used as a final wood finish.

Finishing food utensils

Bowls, spoons, scoops, butter molds, and other wooden household items will come in contact with food, and will encounter washing, hot water, and detergents. When finishing these items, use an edible vegetable oil such as corn oil, soy bean oil, or peanut oil. Don't use varnish! It will peel. Flakes of varnish add little to a tossed salad.

Framing

If your design is not free standing, a frame might well round off your statement. In the chapter on design, we saw how a frame could lend balance to a completely asymmetrical piece. Framing, then, can complete your statement, as well as be part of it.

Chair by Joseph Rodd. Laminated wood. Photo courtesy of The American Craftsman's Council.

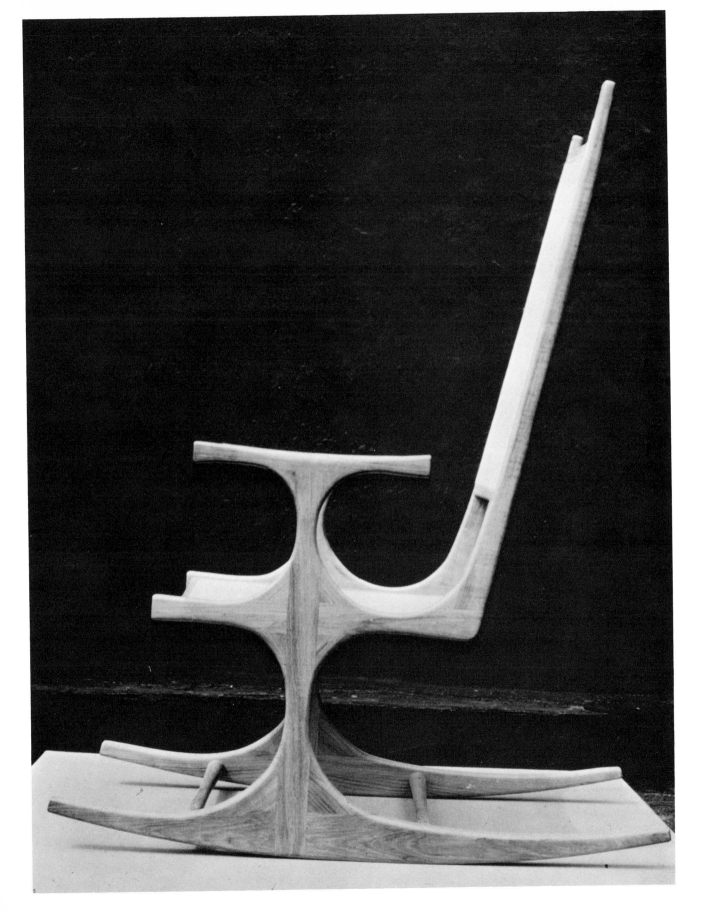

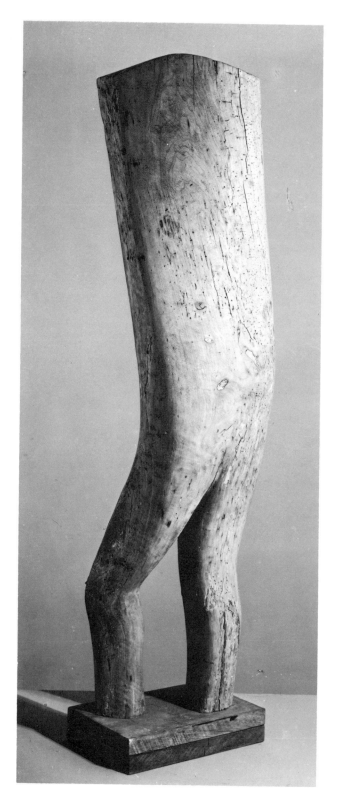

A design can be framed by attaching a frame, as illustrated on page 92. You can also make a frame that is carved as an integral part of the design, as illustrated on page 93. You might mount your design against a background of wood or other material, as illustrated on page 58. I've even seen wall reliefs framed with heavy hemp rope for a nautical effect. Corny, maybe, but it worked on those particular designs.

Signature

Sign your design! Who knows, you may end up writing a book on wood design? But don't sign it all across the face of the design; that is, unless you turn your signature into a sculpture.

Care of finished work

Keep your piece waxed, or well oiled to reduce future cracks and splits. And please . . . blow the dust off it once in awhile!

Ohayo wormy butternut by Raoul Hague, 1947-48. 66½" high; Butternut. (*left*) Texture here is inherent in the wood which was finished smooth by the artist. Photo collection, The Museum of Modern Art, New York, Katherine Cornell Fund.

Shelly at the beach by William King. (*right*) 20" high; Pine. Only a suggestion of detail is necessary on this piece to bring home its impact. Hands and feet are deliberately omitted. Photo courtesy Terry Dintenfass Gallery.

126

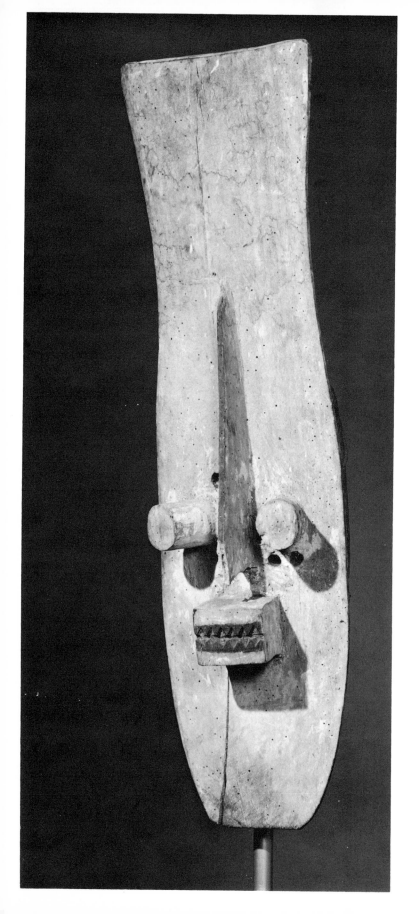

Mask, Liberia, Cape Palmas Region: Grebo. 27½″ high;
painted wood. An example of relief on a functional
design. Photo courtesy The Museum of Primitive Art.

Museum List

Listed below are museums, universities, and historical societies housing extensive collections of wood carvings or holding exhibitions of such work. No matter where you live, there is a collection of wood carvings near you. The list is selective, and by no means includes every collection; a cross-section of the United States and Canada was attempted. Forty-seven states, the District of Columbia, and two Canadian Museums are included in the list. The list is offered as a stimulant for discovering what has been done in the past by designers using wood as their medium. A visit to any one of these institutions is likely to generate a very personal enthusiasm in releasing one's own ideas—at least it does with me.

Alabama

Montgomery Museum of Fine Arts, Montgomery, Alabama.
Tuskegee Institute, George Washington Carver Museum, Tuskegee, Alabama.

Alaska

Alaska Historical Library and Museum, Juneau, Alaska (excellent collection of Indian and Eskimo carvings).
Sheldon Jackson Junior College Museum, Sitka, Alaska (excellent collection of Indian and Eskimo carvings).

Arizona

Prescott Historical Society, Sharlot Hall Museum, Prescott, Arizona.
Phoenix Art Museum, Phoenix, Arizona.
Pioneer's Historical Society, Tucson, Arizona.

Arkansas

University of Arkansas Arts Center Gallery, Fayetteville, Arkansas.

California

University of California, The University Art Gallery, Berkeley, California.
Mission de San Carlos Borromeo de Rio Carmelo, Carmel, California (religious figures carved by California Indians).
Scripps College, Florence Rand Lang Art Gallery, Claremont, California.
La Jolla Museum of Art, La Jolla, California (African and pre-Columbian sculpture).
Los Angeles Art Association, Los Angeles, California.
Los Angeles County Museum of Art, Los Angeles, California.
Ruskin Art Club, Los Angeles, California (engravings).

E. B. Crocker Art Gallery, Sacramento, California.
San Diego Fine Arts Gallery, San Diego, California.
M. H. De Young Memorial Museum, San Francisco, California.
San Francisco Museum of Art, San Francisco, California.
San Gabriel Mission Arcangel, San Gabriel, California.
San Jose State College Art Gallery, San Jose, California.

Colorado

Denver Art Museum, Denver, Colorado.

Connecticut

Marine Historical Association, Mystic, Connecticut (nautical motifs).
Wadsworth Atheneum, Hartford, Connecticut.

Delaware

The Henry Francis DuPont Winterthur Museum, Winterthur, Delaware.
Delaware State Museum, Dover, Delaware.

District of Columbia

National Gallery of Art, Washington, D.C.
Freer Gallery of Art, Washington, D.C.

Florida

Ft. Lauderdale Museum of the Arts, Ft. Lauderdale, Florida.
Cummer Gallery of Art, Jacksonville, Florida.
Dade County Art Museum, Miami, Florida.
Museum of Yesterday's Toys, St. Augustine, Florida.
St. Petersburg Museum of Fine Arts, St. Petersburg, Florida.

Georgia

Atlanta Museum, Atlanta, Georgia.

Hawaii

Honolulu Academy of Arts, Honolulu, Hawaii.

Idaho

Boise Gallery of Art, Boise, Idaho.

Illinois

University of Illinois, Krannert Art Museum, Champaign, Illinois.
The Art Institute of Chicago, Chicago, Illinois.
Chicago Historical Society, Chicago, Illinois.

Indiana

Indiana University Museum of Art, Bloomington, Indiana.
Museum of Arts and Science, Evansville, Indiana.
Ft. Wayne Art Museum, Ft. Wayne, Indiana.

Iowa

Des Moines Art Center, Des Moines, Iowa.
Norwegian-American Historical Museum at Luther College, Decorah, Iowa.
Salisbury House, Des Moines, Iowa.

Kansas

University of Kansas Museum of Art, Lawrence, Kansas.

Kentucky

Louisville Museum, Louisville, Kentucky.

Louisiana

Louisiana State Museum, The Cabildo, New Orleans, Louisiana.

Maine

Bowdoin College Museum of Art, Brunswick, Maine.
Portland Museum of Art, Portland, Maine.

Maryland

The Baltimore Museum of Art, Baltimore, Maryland.
The Walters Art Gallery, Baltimore, Maryland.

Massachusetts

The Bostonian Society, Old State House, Boston, Massachusetts.
Museum of Fine Arts, Boston, Massachusetts.
Old Sturbridge Village, Old Sturbridge, Massachusetts.

Peabody Museum, Salem, Massachusetts.
Worcester Art Museum, Worcester, Massachusetts.
Worcester Historical Society, Worcester, Massachusetts.

Michigan
The Edison Institute, Dearborn, Michigan.

Minnesota
Minnesota Historical Society, St. Paul, Minnesota.
American-Swedish Institute, Minneapolis, Minnesota.
Minneapolis Institute of Art, Minneapolis, Minnesota.
Walker Art Center, Minneapolis, Minnesota.

Mississippi
Mississippi State Historical Museum, Jackson, Mississippi.

Missouri
City Art Museum, St. Louis, Missouri.
Springfield Art Museum, Springfield, Missouri.
William Rockhill Nelson Gallery, Kansas City, Missouri.

Montana
Montana Historical Society, Helena, Montana.

Nebraska
Joslyn Art Museum, Omaha, Nebraska.

Nevada
Nevada Historical Society, Reno, Nevada.

New Hampshire
Saint-Gaudens Museum, Cornish, New Hampshire.
Dartmouth College, The Hopkins Center Art Gallery, Hanover, New Hampshire.

New Jersey
Monmouth County Historical Association, Monmouth, New Jersey.

Montclair Art Museum, Montclair, New Jersey.
The Newark Museum, Newark, New Jersey.
Princeton University, The Art Museum, Princeton, New Jersey.

New York

Brooklyn Museum, Brooklyn, New York.
The Metropolitan Museum of Art, New York, New York.
Museum of Modern Art, New York, New York.
The American Craftsmen's Council, New York, New York.
New York Historical Society, New York, New York.
Museum of Primitive Art, New York, New York.
Guggenheim Museum, New York, New York.
Whitney Museum, New York, New York.
New York State Historical Association, Cooperstown, New York.
State University of New York, Albany, New York.
State University of New York, Buffalo, New York.

North Carolina

University of North Carolina, William Hayes Ackland Memorial Art Center, Chapel Hill, North Carolina.
The Mint Museum of Art, Charlotte, North Carolina.
The North Carolina Museum of Art, Raleigh, North Carolina.

Ohio

The Akron Institute of Art, Akron, Ohio.
Cleveland Museum of Art, Cleveland, Ohio.
The Columbus Gallery of Fine Arts, Columbus, Ohio.

Oklahoma

Oklahoma Art Center, Oklahoma City, Oklahoma.

Oregon

University of Oregon Museum of Art, Eugene, Oregon.
Portland Art Museum, Portland, Oregon.

Pennsylvania

Everhart Museum of Natural History, Science, and Art, Scranton, Pennsylvania.

Bucks County Historical Society, Doylestown, Pennsylvania.
Landis Valley Museum Association, Lancaster, Pennsylvania.
Philadelphia Museum of Art, Philadelphia, Pennsylvania.
University of Pennsylvania Museum, Philadelphia, Pennsylvania.

Rhode Island

King Phillip Museum, Haffenreffer Collection, Mount Hope, Rhode Island.
Newport Historical Society, Newport, Rhode Island.
Rhode Island School of Design, Museum of Art, Providence, Rhode Island.

South Carolina

Carolina Art Association, Gibbs Art Gallery, Charleston, South Carolina.
Florence Museum, Florence, South Carolina.

Tennessee

The Dulin Gallery of Art, Knoxville, Tennessee.
Brooks Memorial Art Gallery, Memphis, Tennessee.

Texas

Dallas Museum of Fine Arts, Dallas, Texas.
Contemporary Arts Association, Houston, Texas.
Marion Koogler McNay Art Institute, San Antonio, Texas.

Utah

University of Utah, Utah Museum of Fine Arts, Salt Lake City, Utah.

Vermont

Shelburne Museum, Shelburne, Vermont.
Vermont Historical Society, Montpelier, Vermont.
Bundy Art Gallery, Waitsfield, Vermont.
Flemming Museum, University of Vermont, Burlington, Vermont.

Virginia

Colonial Williamsburg, Inc., Williamsburg, Virginia.
The Mariners' Museum, Newport News, Virginia.
Virginia Museum of Fine Arts, Richmond, Virginia.

Washington

Seattle Art Museum, Seattle, Washington.

West Virginia

Huntington Galleries, Huntington, West Virginia.

Wisconsin

State Historical Society of Wisconsin, Madison, Wisconsin.
Milwaukee Art Center, Milwaukee, Wisconsin.

Wyoming

Bradford Brinton Memorial Ranch, Big Horn, Wyoming.
Wyoming State Museum, Cheyenne, Wyoming.

Canada

Montreal Museum of Fine Arts, Montreal, Canada.
Nova Scotia College of Art, Museum, Halifax, Nova Scotia.

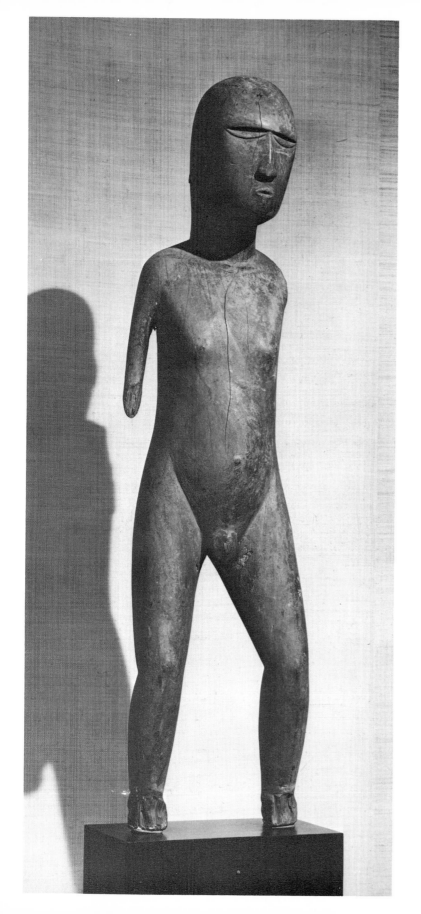

Figure of a god, Polynesia, Gambier Islands, Mangareva. 38¾″ high; wood; eighteenth century. This free standing figure was carved and finished smooth. Photo courtesy The Museum of Primitive Art.

Suggested Reading List

Sculpture

A Concise History of Modern Sculpture, Herbert Read, Praeger, 1965
Contemporary Sculpture, Arts Yearbook 8, The Art Digest, Inc., 1965
Early American Wood Carving, E. O. Christiansen, World Publishing Company 1952
Woodcarving for Beginners, Charles Graveney, Watson-Guptill Publications, 1967
Techniques of Wood Sculpture, Chaim Gross, Arco Publishers, 1964
Sculpture in Wood, John Rood, University of Minnesota, 1950
Woodcarving with Power Tools, Ralph E. Beyer, Chilton Publications, 1959
How to Carve Characters in Wood, H. S. Anderson, University of New Mexico, 1953

Design

The Nature of Design, David Pye, Reinhold Publishing Corporation, 1966
Basic Design, the Dynamics of Visual Form, Maurice de Sausmarez, Studio Vista, 1964
Elements of Design, Donald M. Anderson, Holt, Rinehart, and Winston, 1961
Vision in Motion, L. Moholy-Nagy, Paul Theobald Publishers, 1956
Visual Design, a Problem Solving Approach, Lillian Garrett, Reinhold Publishing Corporation, 1967

Anatomy

Constructive Anatomy, George B. Bridgman, Barnes and Noble, 1966
Dynamic Anatomy, Burne Hogarth, Watson-Guptill Publications, 1958

Furniture

Furniture Treasury (two volumes), Wallace Nutting, The Macmillan Company, 1954

Suppliers' List

A & E Equipment Co., 121 N.W. Third St., Oklahoma City, Okla. 73102

Alexander's Sculptural Supply, 117 East 39th St., N.Y.C., N.Y., tools.

Arts and Crafts Materials Corp., 321 Park Ave., Baltimore, Md. 21201, tools, catalogue.

Art Ellis Paint & Supply, 2508 J St., Sacramento, Calif. 95816

Artsign Materials Co., 2300 Cedar Ave., Minneapolis, Minn. 55404

Atlanta Art Center, 734 West Peachtree, Atlanta, Ga. 30308

Al J. Bader Company, 1113 Locust St., St. Louis, Mo. 63135

Barry Art Supplies, Inc., 114 N. Orange Ave., Sarasota, Fla. 33577

T. E. Binford, Oceanlake, Oregon, native Oregon wood.

Charles F. Bingler, 498 6th Avenue, N.Y.C., N.Y. 10011, English carving tools.

Boin Arts & Crafts Co., 91 Morris St., Morristown, N.J. 07960

David D. Brill, Inc., 1015 Chestnut St., Philadelphia, Penna. 19072

Arthur Brown Bros., 2 West 46 St., New York, N.Y. 10036

I. Michael Brown Co., 15 West 7th St., Erie, Pa. 16509

Brush and Palette, 110 N. Broad St., Kennett Square, Pa. 19348

Buck Brothers, Riverlin Works, Millbury, Mass., woodcarving tools.

James Burnett, 1501 Gaylord St., Long Beach 13, Calif., imported wood.

The Carborundum Co., Niagara Falls, N.Y., abrasives.

Albert Constantine and Sons, Inc., 2050 Eastchester Rd., Bronx, N.Y. 10461, tools and unusual wood, catalogue available.

Cotton-Hanlon, Odessa, N.Y., hardwood and some imported wood.

W. L. Coughty Co., 524 Broadway, Albany, N.Y. 12207

The Craftool Co., 1 Industrial Road, Wood-Ridge, N.J. 07075, tools.

Craftsmans Wood Service Co., 2727 So. Mary St., Chicago, Ill. 60608, wood, catalogue.

Bert L. Daily Inc., 120 E. Third St., Dayton, Ohio 45402

Dixie Art Supplies, Inc., 532 Poydras St., New Orleans, La. 70130

The Dodd Co., 1025 Huron Rd., Cleveland, Ohio 44115

George C. Drury Co., 420 Union St., Nashville, Tenn. 37219

Economy Crafts, Inc., 47–11 Francis Lewis Blvd., Flushing, N.Y. 11361, tools, catalogue.

Educational Lumber Co., Asheville, N.C., wood.

Ettl Studios, Inc., Ettl Lane, Greenwich, Conn. 06830, sculpture supplies, catalogue 25¢.

Favor Ruhl & Watson Co., 121 S. Wabash Ave., Chicago, Ill. 60603

Flax's Artists Materials, 250 Sutter St., San Francisco, Calif. 94108

Sam Flax Inc., 25 East 28th St., New York, N.Y. 10016

The Flax Co., 251 East Grand Ave., Chicago, Ill. 60611

Franklyn Artists' Materials, 2326 West Seventh St., Los Angeles, Calif. 90057

Franklin Glue Co., Columbus, Ohio, woodworking glue.

Fredrix Artists Materials, 140 Sullivan Street, N.Y.C., N.Y. 10012, tools, catalogue.

A. I. Friedman, 25 W. 45th St., New York, N.Y. 10036

Gager's Handicraft Co., 1024 Nicollet Ave., Minneapolis, Minn. 55401

Garth Artist Supply Co., 1513 Broadway, Detroit, Mich. 48226

Gaston Finishes, Bloomington, Ind., stains, finishes, and accessories.

General Finishes, Sales and Svc., 1548 West Bruce St., Milwaukee, Wis. 53240, finishes.

Georgia-Pacific Corp., P.O. Box 311, Portland, Oregon 97207, wood.

Grand Central Art Materials, 3 East 40 St., New York, N.Y. 10016

H. and H. Grinding Co., 2127 East 2nd Street, Cleveland, Ohio, tool sharpening.

J. L. Hammett Co., 2393 Vauxhall Road, Union, N.J. 07083

Hatfield's Color Shop Inc., 859 Boyleston St., Boston, Mass. 02130

Haycor's, 345 106th Ave. N.E., Bellevue, Wash. 98004

Heidl Slocum Co., 95 Chambers St., N.Y.C., N.Y. 10008, sculpture supplies.

Holt and Bugbee, 243 Medford, Boston, Mass., imported wood and other hardwood.

William Hunrath Co., Inc., 153 East 57th St., N.Y.C., N.Y. 10022, furniture, hardware, and frame hangers.

Hyannis Art Supplies, 13 Sherman Square, Hyannis, Mass. 02601

Johnson Artist Materials Inc., 355 Newbury St., Boston, Mass. 02115

R. T. Jones Lumber Co., 1805 Elmwood Avenue, Buffalo, N.Y., hardwood and imports.

Knape and Vogt Mfg., 658 Richmond St., N.W. Grand Rapids, Mich., furniture hardware.

Koenig Art Shop Inc., 166 Fairfield Ave., Bridgeport, Conn. 06603

Leitz Co., 330 Corey Way, San Francisco, Calif. 94080, wood.

M. D. Lee Tool Company, Irondequoit Branch, Rochester 17, N.Y., tools.

Leslie's Art Supplies, 2220 W. Seventh St., Los Angeles, Calif. 90057

Lewis Artist Supply Co., 6408 Woodward Ave., Detroit, Mich. 48202

Logans, Inc., 1836 North High St., Columbus, Ohio 43201

Kenneth Lynch and Sons, 78 Danbury Rd., Wilton, Conn., gallery supplies, catalogue.

Minnesota Woodworkers Supply Co., 925 Winnetka North, Minneapolis, Minn. 55427, tools, furniture hardware, catalogue available.

Frank Mittermeier, Inc., 3577 E. Tremont Ave., Bronx, N.Y. 10465, sculpture supplies.

J. H. Monteath Lumber Co., 2500 Park Ave., N.Y.C., N.Y., wood, catalogue available.

Morse Graphic Art Supply Co., 1938 Euclid, Cleveland, Ohio 44115

George F. Muth Co., 1332 New York Ave. N.W., Washington, D.C. 20005

Nasco House of Crafts, 1271 Gillingham Road, Neenah, Wis. 54956, tools, catalogue.

N.Y. Central Supply Co., 62 Third Ave., New York, N.Y. 10003

Norton Company, Worcester 6, Mass., abrasives.

Reddi Arts Supply, 1225 Hendricks Ave., Jacksonville, Fla. 32207

Rex Art Supply, 2263 S.W. 37th Ave., Miami, Fla. 33145

Sandvik Steel, Inc., 1702 Nevins Road, Fair Lawn, N.J., tools.

San Jose Paint & Wallpaper Co., 112 So. 2nd St., San Jose, Calif. 95113

Sax Arts and Crafts, P.O. Box 2002, Milwaukee, Wis. 53201, tools, catalogue available.

Sculpture Associates, 114 East 25th Street, N.Y.C., N.Y. 10010, wood, tools, catalogue.

Sculpture House, Inc., 38 East 30th St., N.Y.C., N.Y. 10036, wood, tools and free catalogue.

Sculpture Services, Inc., 9 East 19th St., N.Y.C., N.Y., sculpture supplies, catalogue 25¢.

Stewart Industries, 6520 N. Hoyne Ave., Chicago, Ill. 60645, wood.

Otto Ulbrich Co. Inc., 446 Main St., Buffalo, N.Y. 14202

United Artist Materials Co., 32 W. 53 St., New York, N.Y. 10019

U.S. General Supply Corp., 299 Broadway, N.Y.C., N.Y. 10007, tools, catalogue available.

J. D. Wallace and Co., 800 No. Detroit St., Warsaw, Indiana, woodworking machinery.

Webcraft, Inc., Bridgeport, Conn., webbing, cotton, jute, and plastic for chairs.

Weil-Armistead, P.O. Box 214, 900 S. Perry St., Montgomery, Ala. 36101

H. L. Wild, 510 East 11th St., N.Y.C., N.Y. 10009, wood and tools.

Woodworkers Tool Works, 222–224 S. Jefferson St., Chicago, Ill. 60606, tools, catalogue.

X-Acto, Inc., 48-41 Van Dam St., Long Island City, N.Y. 11101, disposable blade tools and knives, free catalogue.

Index

Edited by Susan E. Meyer
Designed by James Craig
Drawings by Sandy Willcox
Composed in eleven point Electra by Atlantic Linotype Co.
Printed and bound by The Haddon Craftsmen, Inc.

DATE DUE

FEB - 8 '76			
MAR - 7 '76			
APR - 4 '76			
SEP 1 9 '76			
FEB 5 '78			
DEC 2 1 1979			
JAN 31 1980			
DEC 1 7 1980			
MAR 5 1981			
APR 2 6 '85			
APR 0 1 1990			

GAYLORD — PRINTED IN U.S.A.